MASTER
WRISTWATCHES

By CAROLINE CHILDERS
and ROBERTA NAAS

BW Publishing Associates, Inc.
IN ASSOCIATION WITH
Rizzoli International Publications, Inc.

MASTER WRISTWATCHES

First published in the United States of America in 1999 by

Ms. Caroline Childers
and BW Publishing Associates, Inc.
11 W. 25th Street New York, NY 10010

IN ASSOCIATION WITH
Rizzoli International Publications, Inc.
300 Park Avenue South, New York, NY 10010

ISBN 0-8478-2192-7
LIBRARY OF CONGRESS CATALOG CARD NUMBER 98-68533

CHAIRMAN

Joseph Zerbib

CHIEF EXECUTIVE OFFICER AND PUBLISHER

Caroline Childers

PRESIDENT

Yael Choukroun

SENIOR VICE PRESIDENT

Esther Tavor

EDITOR

Natalie Warady

Birth of the Wristwatch, After Eight, Dawn of a New Era and Winning Time chapters written by Roberta Naas.

Disclaimer: The information contained in Master Wristwatches has been provided by third parties. While we believe that these sources are reliable, we assume no responsibility or liability for the accuracy of technical details contained in this book.

Every effort has been made to locate the copyright holders of materials used in this book. Should there be any errors or omissions, we apologize and shall be pleased to make acknowledgments in future editions.

Logo by Danielle Loufrani

Printed in Hong Kong

FRONT AND BACK COVER Patek Philippe's complicated wristwatch, ref. 5059, truly combines advanced technology with the elegance of a long lost era. The self-winding, retrograde perpetual calendar movement with moon phases is housed in an 18K yellow gold case reminiscent of the hunter-style pocket watches of the last century. By opening the cover of the caseback, the exquisite movement can be viewed through a sapphire crystal. The hand-finished movement took highly skilled craftsmen almost two years to complete and is hallmarked with the Geneva Seal.

PREVIOUS PAGE Gents' Automatic "Memory Time" wristwatch with a second time zone. Case in platinum with a genuine sapphire cabochon. Parmigiani.

FACING PAGE Men's watch in 18K yellow gold in the classic tonneau style with an automatic movement, power reserve indicator, date and small second hand. Chopard.

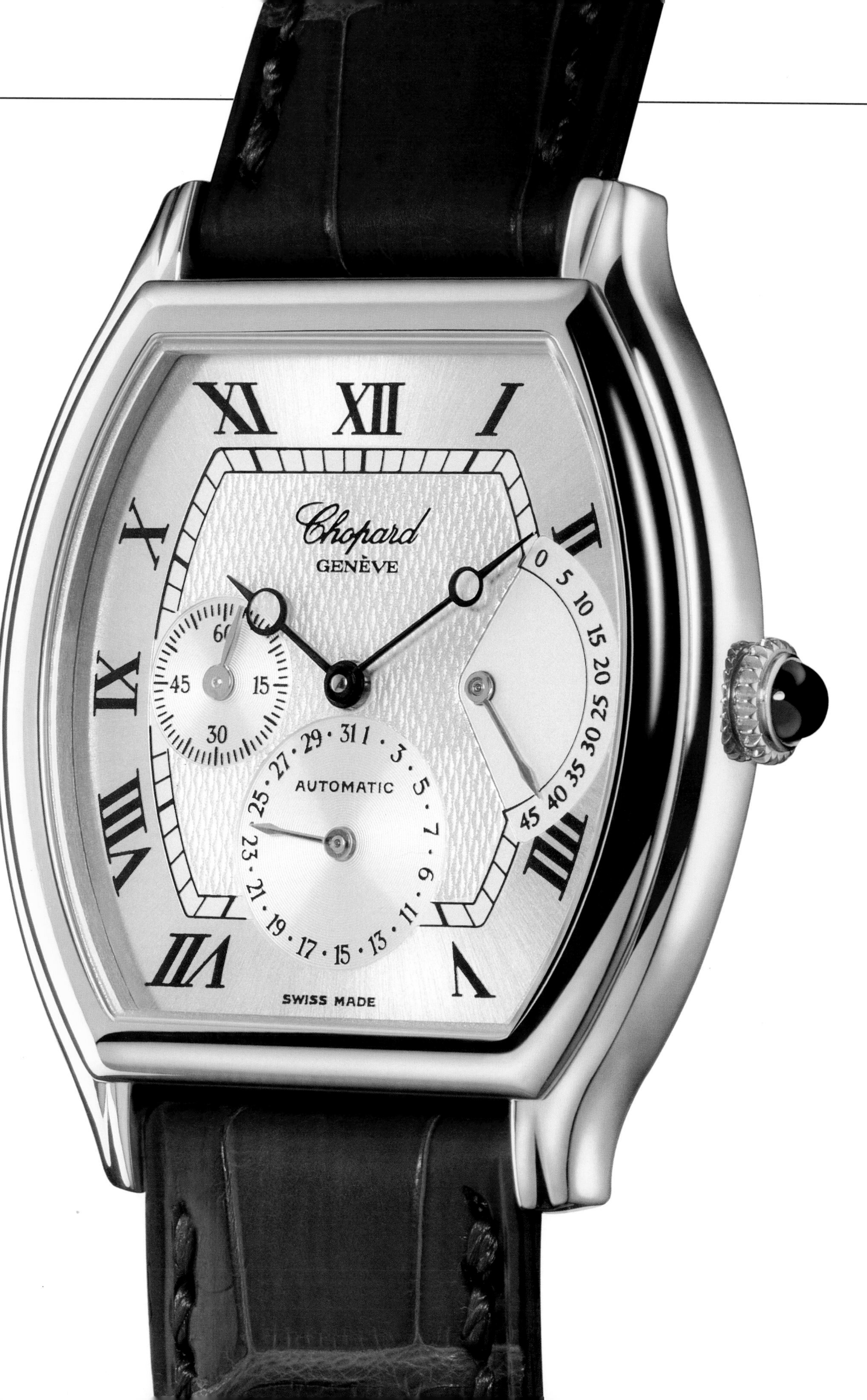
Chopard
GENÈVE
AUTOMATIC
SWISS MADE

CONTENTS

FACING PAGE Extreme refinement is the hallmark of this new President Tourbillon with Three Gold Bridges, with its grand complication and classic lines. Girard-Perregaux.

With each new advance in technology comes a rise in the demands on our time. Urgent deadlines and frequent communication with people in locations all over the world make us increasingly dependent on accuracy and the additional functions that can help keep pace with modern life. And today's watchmakers, much like their predecessors from decades earlier, strive to address man's changing needs. For example, some companies offer watches that tell the hour in three time zones, a special feature that is particularly useful for today's bankers who must keep abreast of markets in Tokyo, London and New York.

The three time zone feature is one of many specialized functions that watchmakers incorporate with the wristwatch, a relatively new innovation itself. The wristwatch is less than one hundred years old and the myriad of advancements, including the development of quartz, has allowed us to rely on our wristwatch without a second thought.

In recent history, man was happy if his watch worked at all. Today, we enjoy the benefit of hundreds of years of developments that keep us on time and allow us to track time to the smallest of fractions. This book celebrates all of the great names and advancements that have put precision onto the wrist.

CAROLINE CHILDERS

FACING PAGE Hublot chronoraph wristwatch, case in 18K yellow gold, water-resistant to 100m (330 feet).

This book could not have been produced without the assistance and kindness of many people who generously shared with us their knowledge and experience of the watchmaking industry. We want to thank Mr. Peter Laetsch, President of the Federation of the Swiss Watch Industry in America, and his wife Sylvia for their enduring friendship and support. We want to express our gratitude to all the individuals and companies who devoted their time and patience: Mr. Maurice Altermatt of the Federation Horlogere; Mr. Joe Thompson, President of America Time; Mr. Marc Junod from Audemars Piguet, USA; Ms. Pauline Bochot from Audemars Piguet, Switzerland; Mr. Christian Bedat from Bedat & Co.; Genéve; Mr. Gerard Pichon-Varin from Boucheron, New York; Ms. Murielle Blanchard, Mr. Alain Boucheron from Boucheron, Paris; Ms. Béatrice Vuille from Breguet, Switzerland; Ms. Valerie Burgat from Breitling, Switzerland; Ms. Anne Walle from Breitling, USA; Ms. Julie Keating from Cartier, USA; Ms. Caroline Gruosi-Scheufele, Ms. Annick Benoit-Godet from Chopard, Genéve; Ms. Jeanne Massaro, Ms. Diana Moran, Mr. Harry Viola, Ms. Livia Marotta, Mr. John Rooney from Concord; Ms. Andrea V. Suriano from Daniel Roth, New York; Ms. Katie Kinsella from Franck Muller, USA, Ms. Cristina D'Agostino from Franck Muller, Switzerland; Ms. Andrea V. Suriano from Gerald Genta, New York; Mr. Luigi Macaluso, Ms. Sylvie Rumo, Ms. Jacqueline Briggen from Girard-Perregaux, Switzerland; Mr. Ronald Jackson from Girard-Perregaux, USA; Ms. Linda Passaro, Ms. Missy Roxas from Hamilton, USA; Mr. Carlo Crocco, Ms. Véronique Kandaouroff from Hublot, Switzerland; Mr. Ed Suhyda from Hublot, USA; Mr. Michael Benavente, Ms. Janet Cerruti from Longines, USA; Mr. Nicolas Hayek from Swatch Group, Switzerland; Mr. Venanzio Ciampa from Omega-Swatch Group, Switzerland; Ms. Anne Biéler from Parmigiani, Switzerland; Ms. Tania Edwards from Patek Philippe, New York; Ms. Pamela Cloutier, Mr. Hugues-Olivier Borès from Patek Philippe, Switzerland; Mr. Jean Siegenthaler from Editions Scriptar S.A. for the use of *Watchmaking: History, Art and Science* by Catherine Cardinal and *Masterpieces of Watchmaking* by Luigi Pippa. We would also like to give special thanks to Frenchway Travel, who make the impossible mission, possible.

CAROLINE CHILDERS

FACING PAGE Bedat & Co. bracelet watch from collection number 3, set with 594 diamonds on steel.

Our most heartfelt thanks are extended to
Mr. Joseph Zerbib, a tireless source of strength
who supported us every step of the way and without whom
MASTER WRISTWATCHES *would not be possible.*

To my children

For over 200 years, Swiss craftsmen have devoted themselves to creating the perfect timepiece. At the Federation of the Swiss Watch Industry, the only trade organization that represents watches, we promote this tradition and the reputation that has been built and upheld over many generations. There is always a demand for high quality watches. Quartz electronic devices have become popular for their sleek design and simple function; however, they do have limitations in terms of their reparability. Mechanical watches, on the other hand, can remain in families for future generations. Men are often particularly intrigued by the mechanics of complicated watches, while women are more interested in the aesthetics. The appeal of a timepiece — and the popularity of classic watch styles — is affected by advances in technology far less than are other mechanical devices. For instance, there is little nostalgia for — let alone actual use of — mechanical typewriters, yet mechanical watches have a unique appeal that remains constant. There is a romance to the act of recapturing the past by gracing the wrist with a bejeweled timepiece. America is the largest market for Swiss watches. Many American consumers own several watches to suit their varying needs, and we attempt to guide them in understanding the complex choices available to them. Through books such as this one, the public is informed about the evolution of modern timepieces and can see the array of innovative designs before them.

Peter Laetsch
PRESIDENT
Federation of the Swiss Watch Industry, New York

WATCHES HAVE A SOUL, THEIR MESSAGE MUST BE WARMHEARTED AND POSITIVELY EMOTIONAL. As the world's leader of watchmaking, we at the Swatch Group are well aware of these assets. This is the reason why all our brands have their own unmistakable message, from the luxury and top brands — Blancpain, Omega, Rado and Longines — over the middle range — Tissot, Calvin Klein, Certina, Mido, Pierre Balmain and Hamilton — down to the basic segment with Swatch, FlikFlak, Lanco and the private label sector, Endura.

One of the main reasons why we have changed our former name SMH Swiss Corporation for Microelectronics and Watchmaking Industries into the simpler Swatch Group was certainly emotion. What do the three letters SMH evoke? Outstanding quality? High tech? Art? Emotion? Beauty? Warmheartedness? For some it might, for most it won't. But this is what the Swatch Group is all about.

We were looking for a name which was known and legally usable internationally. That's why Swatch was our choice. Did you know that Swatch is counted among the ten most renown brands of the world? And to tell you all, the Swatch Group would probably not have reconquered its number one position without the Swatch watch.

In the early eighties, when the Swiss watch industry lived disastrous moments, I was asked by Swiss bankers to analyze the situation of the two Swiss watch giants SSIH and Asuag. As you are all aware of, I recommended to merge the two concerns and to strengthen the position of the new Group by creating a new brand, and emotional mass consumer product — Swatch.

Everybody expected us to attack our Far Eastern competitors in the upper market segment. But one of my theses is that you can only defend the upper market segment if you control the lower market segment — for the following main reasons:

MASS BRINGS MASS. If you are wearing your watch, you cannot avoid that during one year between 3000 to 5000 people see this watch. 0.3% of these people might well want, according to our experience, to buy this same watch. Up today, we have sold approximately 250 million Swatch watches since 1983.

MASS PRODUCTION ALLOWS YOU to automate your production lines and procedures and permits you to buy sophisticated and high-quality tools for all your products — hence high quality and lower production costs.

IF YOUR CUSTOMER gets used to a brand when he is young and does not have much money, he will continue to buy your brand when he is older, better off and able to spend more money.

FINALLY, IF YOU ATTACK the lower and middle market segment, you hinder your competitor to get into the upper market segment, because he is forced to act in the same segment in order to not lose market shares.

Swatch is one of the great timepieces of the world. Because it is the foundation of the Swatch Group watch brands. That is why none of our brands were, when consulted, opposed to the new name. But, of course, Swatch is much more than just an emotional mass consumer product. It is the successful marriage between watch and art, between watch and fashion, between high-tech and watchmaking craftsmanship. It is a worthy sister of Blancpain, where you will never find a quartz watch, or Omega, whose primary choice in 1999 will be the Speedmaster and the 30th anniversary of lunar landing. Or of Rado, the watch for people challenging the future, and of Longines, reflecting the elegance of time.

The watch industry is an important element of the Swiss economy. "Bubbling", in fact inflating values of shares on the stock exchange do not add any additional real wealth and value nor one single job to our industry or to our economy unless new products and new wealth have been created before. And only new products create new jobs. It is therefore essential not only for the Swiss economy, but also for the European economy to multiply our efforts and keep on creating, innovating and producing new products.

Nicolas G. Hayek
CHAIRMAN AND CEO
The Swatch Group
Biel, November 16, 1998

In this hectic, fast-paced world, time can seem like an illusion. In daily business, schedules are constantly juggled, arranged and rearranged. Meeting times are set and then completely altered. Often we act from one day to the next based on plans set out months in advance. And each day — to restore reality to this illusion — we glance regularly, instinctively at the watches on our wrists to note the hour, to see how much time is left before we start or finish some important task. One hundred years ago, one did not have the luxury of that quick and easy glance toward the wrist. One had to reach for a pendant watch hung around the neck, or pull out a pocket watch from one's vest to check the progress of that fleeting time. Wristwatches — now such a common element in the everyday wardrobe that they are taken for granted — can boast barely a century of history. It is only fitting that the Swiss watchmakers — with their centuries-long tradition of craftsmanship and innovation in timekeeping — were the ones to introduce the concept of the wristwatch. Despite their token appearances during the late 1700s and early 1800s, wristwatches truly became established only around the turn of the century — and even then, they were viewed as the odd outsider. It was during World War I that the wristwatch was finally able to demonstrate its superior ease of use and firmly establish the rationale for its existence. With the end of the war, wristwatches reached their full glory as the preferred means of personal timekeeping. Throughout the remaining decades of the twentieth century, the wristwatch has undergone further progress and change. With the technological advances, financial crises and major wars of the century, different countries have by turn emerged and retreated as watchmaking powers. America, Europe and the Far East

all at various times have been in the forefront of watchmaking during the course of the last hundred years. This book outlines the century of the wristwatch. The first chapter, "Birth of the Wristwatch," describes the historical acceptance of the mechanical wristwatch, the invention of the automatic, or self-winding wristwatch, the creation of water-resistant wristwatches, the development of thinner and flatter wristwatch movements, the first quartz watch and the rise of the quartz movement, which would forever change wristwatch history. While the majority of these innovations came first from the Swiss, not all did. This chapter touches, as well, on some of the countries involved in wristwatch development throughout the decades, and the technological, economic and political factors that influenced wristwatch making, delineating the contributions of each important watchmaking nation. "Dawn of a New Era" describes the introduction of quartz wristwatches to the world, with a look at the various countries that took part in their creation and the impact they had on both the power and financial success of the watchmaking companies involved and on the fashion world in general. "Winning Time" traces the growth of the sport wristwatch category, and "After Eight" details the creative genius and painstaking labor behind the creation of the high-jeweled wristwatch. Throughout the century, a great number of technological developments have made an impact on the wristwatch industry. Still, while a variety of new gadgets and gizmos have become part of even moderately priced wristwatches, and while quartz has revolutionized both the science and the art of precision timekeeping, it remains as true today as it was a hundred years ago, that the Swiss watchmaking industry — with its mechanical wristwatch wonders, complicated marvels and high-end quartz wristwatch designs — reigns supreme, bringing the world an unrivaled array of master wristwatches.

Roberta Naas

ROBERTA NAAS

FACING PAGE Double-Face Tourbillon by Daniel Roth. Yellow gold with ruthenium silvered dial, in blue steel.

BIRTH OF THE WRISTWATCH

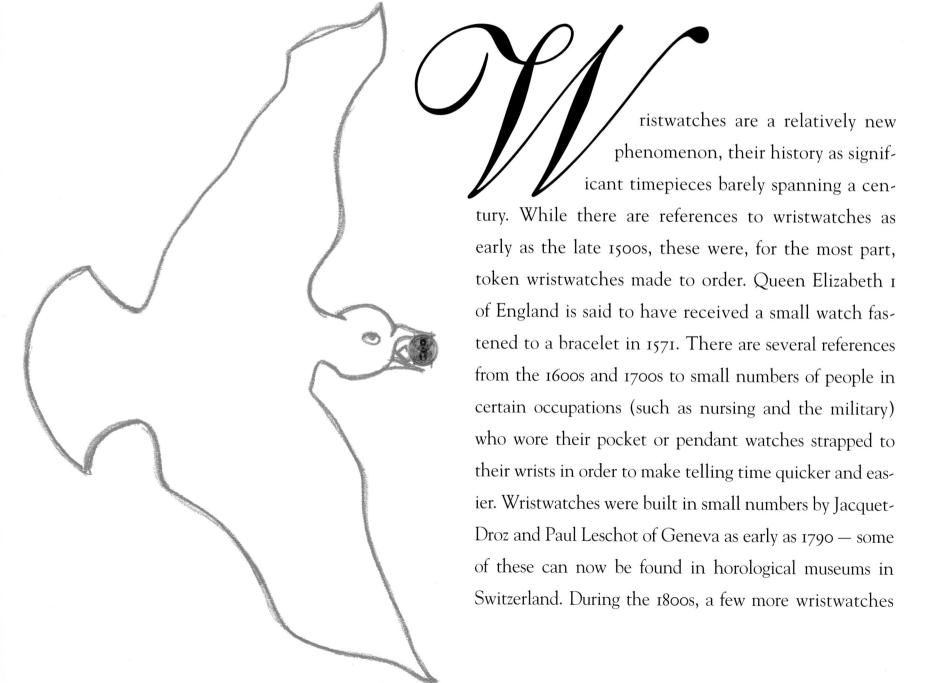

Wristwatches are a relatively new phenomenon, their history as significant timepieces barely spanning a century. While there are references to wristwatches as early as the late 1500s, these were, for the most part, token wristwatches made to order. Queen Elizabeth 1 of England is said to have received a small watch fastened to a bracelet in 1571. There are several references from the 1600s and 1700s to small numbers of people in certain occupations (such as nursing and the military) who wore their pocket or pendant watches strapped to their wrists in order to make telling time quicker and easier. Wristwatches were built in small numbers by Jacquet-Droz and Paul Leschot of Geneva as early as 1790 — some of these can now be found in horological museums in Switzerland. During the 1800s, a few more wristwatches

appeared on the scene. In 1810, Breguet created a repeater wristwatch for the Queen of Naples and in 1838, delivered various small watches with "armbands" to customers. Similarly, Boucheron, Chaumet, Cartier and several other jewelry and watch companies created special timepieces for select royalty in the 1800s.

In 1839, Georges-Auguste Leschot and Pierre-Frederic Ingold introduced the first machines that were capable of manufacturing parts with precision, a step that would eventually lead to factory production of pieces that previously were entirely hand-made. But the Swiss did not fully embrace the machine age until close to the turn of the century. In 1876, the Swiss watchmaking industry sent delegates to the Philadelphia World Exhibition where they were shocked to learn of the American watch industry's strength. Nearly overtaken by the huge strides

OPENING PAGE The view of the craftsmanship involved in the 1957 Perpetual Calendar by Audemars Piguet.

PREVIOUS PAGE Perpetual Calendar by Audemars Piguet created in 1957.

ABOVE Chaumet created these emerald and pearl bracelet wristwatches in 1811 for the Princess of Bavaria.

FACING PAGE LEFT Early wristwatches appealed mostly to women, and were considered another form of jewelry. This floral designed ladies' watch from Patek Philippe, circa 1912, is set with faceted diamonds against an 18K gold bracelet and case.

TOP RIGHT The first IWC wristwatch was created around 1900 and featured a sub seconds hand.

BOTTOM RIGHT Girard-Perregaux made its first wristwatches in 1880 for officers of the German Imperial Navy that were similar in design to this model.

the American watch industry had made in mass production processes, Switzerland embarked on industrialization.

The Swiss recognized that while production of high-end watches could continue to be done by hand by watchmakers and artisans, the industry as a whole had to adapt to mechanization, especially in the production of watches for the more affordable price range. Taking the concept of utilizing machines to mass-produce watches that had been introduced by Ingold and Leschot earlier in the century, the Swiss introduced standardization to its watch industry; by the turn of the new century, increased productivity and interchangeability of parts had brought Switzerland to a reigning position in world watch production. Over time, miniaturization and other technological advances had made

it possible for watches to be efficiently manufactured in sizes suitable for the wrist.

Patek Philippe produced a bracelet with a "built-in" watch in 1868, and in 1880 Girard-Perregaux produced a line of wristwatches with a protective metal grid-work cover over the dial for members of the German Navy.

In 1893, Audemars Piguet developed ladies' wristwatches and some men's units, but not before extensive discussion about whether the winding and setting crown should be on the right or left side of the case: at that time it was not known which wrist people would wear their watches on. It was finally decided that since most people were right-handed the preference would be to wear the watch on the left hand. In 1905, the first wristwatches to go into series production at Audemars Piguet had the crown on the right side for easy access.

By the turn of the century, wristwatches had become important in various professions, particularly the military. In the South African Boer wars of 1899–1902, military officers wore wristwatches as an indispensable part of their field equipment—the ability to read the time by a quick look at the wrist instead of having to go into the pocket for a watch made a critical difference.

ABOVE Movado's Polyplan watches in curved, tonneau-shapes, created in 1915 and crafted in 18K white gold, were indicative of early womens' wristwatches.

ABOVE RIGHT In the 1920s, art deco wristwatches emerged in a myriad of styles for women. This Concord ladies' strap watch from 1924 features an elongated case crafted in platinum and intricately set with diamonds.

RIGHT Piguet's first skeleton wristwatch, 1937.

*D*espite the use of wristwatches in military campaigns, the average man did not embrace the concept of wristwatches. Many men considered them effeminate and scorned the wearing of them. It was women who more often looked to the wristwatch as

something new, different and refreshing; women whose interest in and demand for wristwatches would eventually lead to a broader cultural impact in the twentieth century.

For the wristwatch, the first decade of the century was one of turmoil. It was embraced by some and ignored by others. But, as with many innovations, people gradually began to pay more attention. In 1904, Brazilian aviation pioneer Alberto Santos-Dumont expressed to Cartier his desire for a watch for the wrist to avoid the inconvenience while flying of grappling with a pocket watch. Cartier promptly created the Santos, which today remains one of Cartier's most popular wristwatch designs.

New inventions in wristwatch technology also brought attention. In 1908, Eterna won a patent for the first wristwatch with an alarm mechanism, though the watch was not officially launched for six more years. The first chronograph wristwatch (a separate device that allows timing of intervals, such as laps, etc.) was introduced in 1909—fortuitous timing. Just around the corner was the onset of World War 1. With it came a burst of interest in wristwatches and chronographs that would

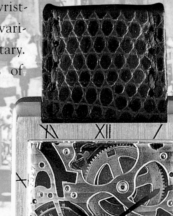

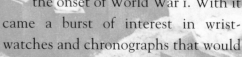

leave an indelible mark on their development. Following the lead role wristwatches had played in the Prussian and Boer wars, governments around the world became increasingly interested in their usefulness. Military officers, aviators and their superiors recognized the crucial advantage offered by watches on the wrist. Orders poured into watch manufacturers in droves. The long-term success of the wristwatch was now certain.

With this growing demand for wristwatches for wartime, several important design directions emerged. Watch manufacturers such as Omega, Movado and Heuer were among the first to introduce chronograph wristwatches and rugged military timepieces. These were also the first manufacturers to create metal grids for military watches that protected the watch crystal and dial but still allowed for easy viewing. These grids later became fashion statements in their own right. Luminous hands and markers became important features (though early processes to

TOP LEFT These 1914 wristwatch models from Eterna were among the first to have an alarm.

TOP RIGHT American pilots synchronise their watches at a USAF airbase before take-off.

ABOVE These classic Cartier Tank watches were popular in the 1940s.

LEFT This Movado wristwatch chronometer, circa 1914, features a protective metal grid for the field of battle.

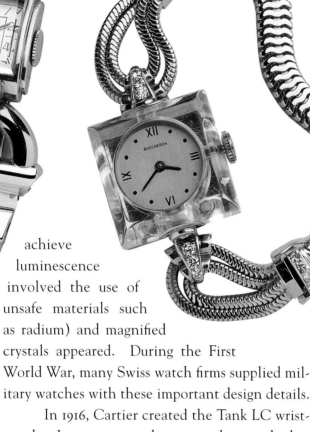

achieve luminescence involved the use of unsafe materials such as radium) and magnified crystals appeared. During the First World War, many Swiss watch firms supplied military watches with these important design details.

In 1916, Cartier created the Tank LC wristwatch. It was a rugged, rectangular watch that was fashioned after the first armored combat vehicle. The watch was given to General Pershing, commander of the American troops in France, and Cartier officially began creating the Tank watch for production and sales three years later. (Today the Tank watch is a signature series for Cartier.)

These first wristwatches were mechanical timepieces that were manually wound by the wearer. The concept of the mechanical watch goes back more than seven hundred years, and the mechanical wristwatch is built on this same philosophy, with many inventions and innovations incorporated along the way.

Generally, a mechanical watch is comprised of approximately 130 different parts. The

mechanical movement consists of a frame, or mainplate, and its moving parts, such as the barrel and the mainspring, a motor, wheel train, escapement system and balance. Once the stem has been turned and the spring mechanism (the energy source) is manually wound, the mechanical movement uses a series of springs, levers and gearwheels to transmit the power. Complicated timepieces—ones that include functions beside timekeeping, such as moon phase, date, alarm, chronograph, retrograde, minute repeater, tourbillon, etc.—naturally are composed of many more parts; some house as many as 700 individual pieces.

As watchmakers strove to reduce watch sizes, and improve complications and other features, the self-winding mechanical watch emerged on the scene. Rather than requiring the wearer to hand-wind the spring, the self-winding watch essentially winds itself via an oscillating weight that is powered by the wearer's movements. The first self-winding watch was created by Abraham-Louis Perrelet around 1770, and it laid the groundwork for all future

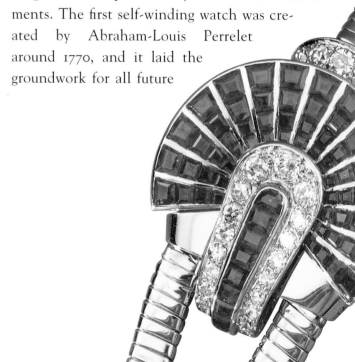

automatic watches. This first self-winding watch, of course, was a pocket watch. Self-winding would come to wristwatches only a century-and-a-half later.)

In 1922, Leon Leroy, a watchmaker from Paris, was inspired by the concept of perpetual motion to create a small series of self-winding wristwatches for an individual client, though they were never produced in quantity. It is English watchmaker John Harwood who is credited with having invented the automatic watch: he was the first to pursue a concept of series (or mass) production—making his efforts the starting point for further development.

*I*n 1923, Harwood applied for patents in Germany, Switzerland and the United States for his self-winding watch, and six years later Harwood's self-winding series production began in earnest. These wristwatches were characterized by their rectangular shape within which the automatic winding movement fit snugly. Unfortunately, they were known to have technical imperfections and were somewhat unreliable in their timekeeping. The Harwood watches would be produced for only a couple of years due to the worldwide economic crisis of the era. Despite the near-misses and the outright failures, watchmakers continued to pursue the concept of the self-winding or automatic wristwatch, but they would not begin to appear in quantity in watch-

makers' lines until the late 1930s and early 1940s.

With the close of World War 1, the rugged styling of the chronographs and military wristwatches caught on with the general public and wristwatches at last became the preferred means of personal timekeeping. In the 1920s, men preferred sporty chronographs, often equipped with multiple functions. Women looked toward elegant, refined, art deco-inspired wristwatches. These women's mechanical watches of the "roaring twenties" were eye-catching in oblong, oval, round, octagon or odd-shaped cases.

Even as it gained in popularity, the technical development and refinement of the wristwatch continued to progress. Among the achievements: shock resistance, water resistance and size reduction. Rolex, which actively sought to perfect the water-resistant wristwatch, made headlines in 1927 when Mercedes Glietze wore her Rolex Oyster watch on her swim across the English Channel. After more than ten hours of submersion under trying conditions, the watch maintained perfect time without condensation or penetration of water. Rolex had succeeded in creating the first water-resistant wristwatch. In 1929, Jaeger-LeCoultre produced the world's smallest movement, the caliber 101—which is still used by the company today.

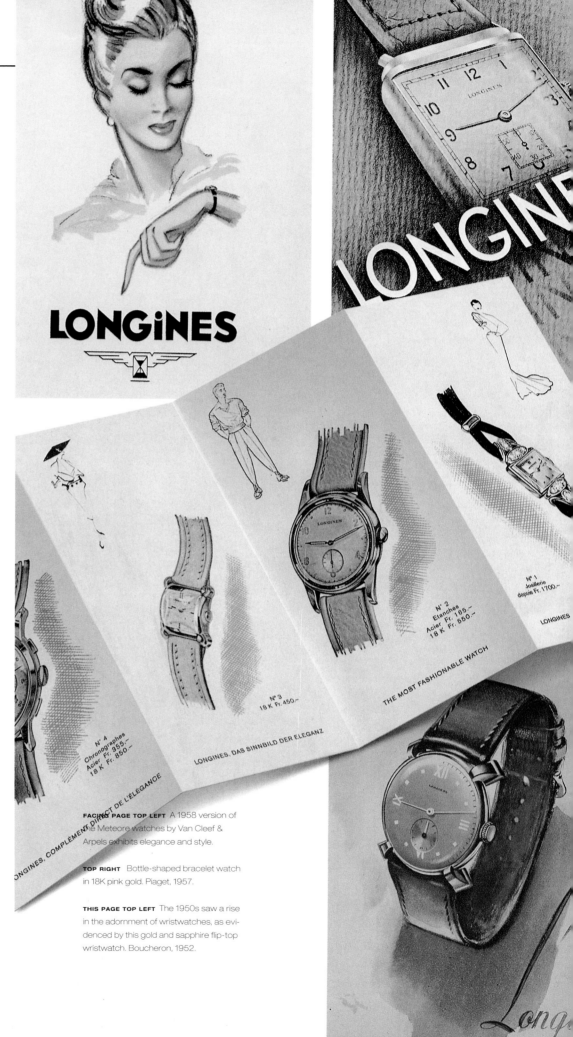

When Black Thursday hit on October 24, 1929, individuals and companies around the world went under. Most businesses that did not collapse, hung on by the barest of margins. Watch companies were not exempt from the disaster. Swiss watchmaking workshops, suffering from lack of orders and sales, were operated with half staffs. Working hours were reduced to several days a week—often watchmakers worked no more than eighty hours a month. Demand for watches dwindled, but even the reduced supply was more than enough to cause rampant deflation, leading many fine watch companies to go out of business. Those that were able to stay afloat, hung on until the worldwide depression ended in 1936.

Watch companies that survived were able to introduce new inventions that had been researched and developed during the depression years. Despite the seemingly quiet watchmaking period of the early 1930s, the mid-1930s reflected some interesting changes, especially in design. As Art Deco continued to dominate design from the twenties into the thirties, women's wristwatches with onyx and marcasite appeared in great numbers. Often these watches were adorned with black silk or satin straps and sometimes sported pearls as well. Geometrical patterns and

FACING PAGE TOP LEFT A 1958 version of the Meteore watches by Van Cleef & Arpels exhibits elegance and style.

TOP RIGHT Bottle-shaped bracelet watch in 18K pink gold. Piaget, 1957.

THIS PAGE TOP LEFT The 1950s saw a rise in the adornment of wristwatches, as evidenced by this gold and sapphire flip-top wristwatch. Boucheron, 1952.

Digital wristwatches became somewhat more prevalent during this decade, as many watch companies introduced special models with digital indications on them. Movado, for instance, introduced rectangular-cased wristwatches with rotating disks to replace the hands, with the time displayed through small apertures in the case.

Still, there would be only a few prosperous years before the onset of World War II would take its toll. By the latter half of the 1930s, German and Japanese expansion were on the rise and so was the demand for precision instruments for impending war. With the onset of World War II, international watch production was both disrupted and fueled. In most countries, on the home fronts, watches were a luxury during

right angles played an important role in designs, as well, as rectangular watch shapes took center stage. As the fine line that identified some watches as functional items and other watches as pieces of jewelry and fashion statements became blurred, design became even more prominent. Many women's watches appeared during this time with covers, or flip-top lids. Experts in this arena include Van Cleef & Arpels, Boucheron and Chanel.

*I*n men's wristwatch designs, practicality was important. It was in the 1930s that Jaeger-LeCoultre invented the Reverso wristwatch, which features a reversible watch. Introduced in 1931 and designed for polo players who needed a way to protect their wristwatches while playing, the Reverso remains the most famous of all Jaeger-LeCoultre watches to this day. Around this time, too, Vacheron Constantin introduced its "Jalousie" timepiece, a watch that featured 18-karat gold shutters over the watch dial that opened and closed with the push of a button to reveal the time.

TOP LEFT Automatic wristwatches became popular in the latter half of the century. Shown here is the Oris Automatic, circa 1952.

TOP RIGHT Tiffany & Co's Queenmatic series of automatic wristwatches for the discerning consumer. This model is circa 1960.

BOTTOM RIGHT These Longines watches from the 1970s depict the bold case designs of the time.

great lengths to conquer the problem of antimagnetism and in 1938, introduced its antimagnetic pilots' watch, the Mark x, which was produced in the 1940s for the British armed forces. The movement of this watch was encased in a soft inner iron ring to deflect magnetic interference. Also in 1938, IWC introduced the oversized Portuguieser watch in response to a request from the Portuguese navy for a large, easily readable wristwatch.

While watches for everyday consumers were indeed considered a luxury, when America entered the war against the Axis powers, American women worked hard to save up for and purchase wristwatches to send to their their husbands and lovers on the front line.

By the second half of the 1940s, the war had ended; family, community and social life was once again in swing. Fashions changed and wristwatches were looked to with renewed interest. Watch styles were fine and elegant. Women's watches were smaller, inspired by classic bracelets and a traditional sense of beauty. Square case shapes were popular among both women and men. Men's watches were also found in round or rectangular shapes, and exhibited a classic elegance of their own.

This post-war period also ushered in the era of television, electronics and technology. The quest was on in all walks of life to improve technology, and the wristwatch was no exception. The next fifteen years of wristwatch development was led primarily by technical advancements in power sources, movement size and the like. Wrist chronometers (watches that are tested under extreme conditions over a period of time for such things as precision, durability, etc., and then certified by the testing organi-

wartime, but on the front lines, watches were a necessity.

The military commands of the war's combatants invested in watches designed specifically for different military specialties, such as fighter pilots and naval saboteurs. While most countries around the world suspended watch manufacturing to devote their resources to war efforts, neutral Switzerland was able to some degree to continue watchmaking during the war, filling many military supply orders. This was the age of true pilot watches, antimagnetic watches and highly water-resistant watches, all geared for precision.

In this decade, Breitling introduced wristwatches with slide rule bezels for pilot calculations and soon became an official supplier of wristwatches for the Royal Air Force. IWC, International Watch Company, went to

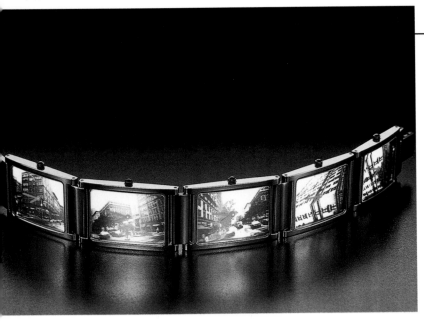

zation) began emerging more prominently, and in 1945 they were added as a category to international chronometer trials and competitions held annually by the Neuchatel and Geneva Observatories. Also playing an increasingly visible role during this time was the wristwatch with calendar.

Watchmakers were introducing efficient, slimmer, more reliable automatic winding systems, finally spurring the rise of the automatic wristwatch. Many fine watch companies introduced their first automatic wristwatches to their lines during this decade, paving the way for others. In 1946 Movado took automatic winding a step further when it introduced the Calendomatic wristwatch, which had a center seconds hand and full calendar function built into it. The calendar featured day and month readout through aperture windows, and the date was shown by a central hand.

Around this time, too, watchmakers began

experimenting with new energy and power sources. In 1948, Eterna introduced the first ball-bearing mounted rotor in a self-winding watch, a standard still used today in automatic wristwatches. The heart of the winding action of the Eterna-Matic, as it was called, was five tiny steel balls. The ball-bearing-mounted winding rotor swings an oscillating weight freely in a complete circle, thereby winding the mainspring at the slightest motion of the hand.

A decade later, in 1957, America's Hamilton Watch Company produced the first electric watch powered by a battery. Ten years in the research and development stage, the electronic watch substituted a battery for the mainspring. While some watch companies jumped on the electronic bandwagon, many Swiss firms stayed true to the mechanical wrist-

thick, making it an ultra-thin movement that could be used in women's watches as well as men's. In 1958, Piaget applied for a patent for an ultra-thin automatic winding device that was aimed at reducing the width of the automatic movement. The final automatic movement was 2.3 mm. The patent was registered the following year and the 12P caliber went on the market. Many of Piaget's watches to this day utilize the 9P and 12P movements.

Watch designs in the 1950s gradually became simpler and cleaner. It was in 1958, in fact, that designer Nathan Horwitt received his patent for a watch dial that was basically absent of any design, markers or numerals. It was a black dial with a simple gold dot at the 12 o'clock position and hour and minute hands. This watch would later become the Museum Watch by Movado. After two years of searching for the right company to create watches using his dial design, Horwitt reached an agreement with Movado, which continues to produce the Museum Watch to this day.

In the 1960s, wristwatches became more lively and fashionable, reflecting the times. This was an era of pop art, the Beatles and mod miniskirts. Watches took on bold new shapes and colors. Creative explosions came from certain companies in particular, such as Piaget, Movado and Omega who utilized a variety of case shapes including octagons, hexagons, ovals and cushioned squares and rectangles. Watches emerged with straps in lavender, teal and a variety of other hues. Additionally, wristwatches of the decade often utilized enamel, semiprecious stones and other materials. Coral, turquoise, lapis lazuli, malachite, jade and tiger eye appeared regularly as dials. In this decade, Corum introduced the

watch. Other technologies also emerged around the same time. Bulova Watch Company, for instance, introduced the first tuning fork watch, called the Accutron. The Accutron uses a tuning fork instead of an escapement to power the oscillating circuit.

This was also an era in which watch manufacturers were dedicating themselves to creating thinner, flatter movements. Every few months one watch company or another would announce the newest, slimmest movements yet devised. Consumers were demanding even more elegant automatic wristwatches and many watch companies set out to achieve further reductions in the size and width of movements. In 1957, Piaget presented the 9P caliber mechanical movement: a thin, flat, refined movement barely two mm

TOP LEFT The mechanical Jaeger-LeCoultre Grand Sport Chronograph wristwatches feature either power reserve or retrograde readout.

TOP RIGHT The Travel Time collection from Patek Philippe. This dual time zone wristwatch features a mechanical handwinding movement with the Geneva Seal Hallmark.

ABOVE The Chronometer Royal, from Vacheron Constantin's Les Historiques collection. Its self-winding mechanical movement provides the date, hours, minutes and seconds, in 18K white gold.

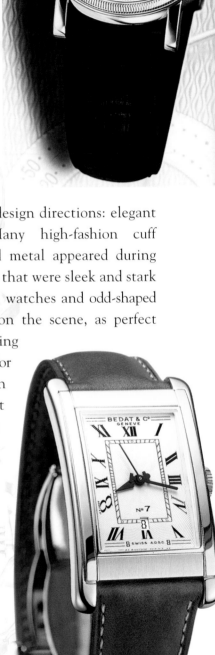

"Coin Watch," which featured a coin as the watch dial, with an ultra-slim movement between the two sides of a gold coin. Corum selected the American gold $20 Double Eagle for its first coin watches, which are still produced today.

Many watch companies were now utilizing ultra-thin mechanical movements for their wristwatches, allowing for greater design freedom. Luxury watch companies focused on gemstone-adorned wristwatches for women and on classically elegant watches for men. Wristwatches without hour markings appeared more frequently from companies such as Movado and Corum. Many important patents were also awarded during this decade, particularly in the field of electric drives and control units.

In 1969, the first automatic chronograph wristwatches were introduced to the world by a group of watchmaking competitors who had been working in concert to achieve this feat, including Breitling, Hamilton-Buren and Heuer. This was also the year that man first walked on the moon. On July 21, 1969, when astronaut Neil Armstrong took that giant leap onto the moon, he was wearing an Omega Speedmaster wristwatch.

The early 1970s saw the introduction of quartz wristwatches (see "Dawn of a New Era" for further discussion), which plunged Switzerland's watch industry into a crisis and affected the future of wristwatch movement preferences around the world. With the rampant unemployment and bankruptcy of many watch firms, assembly lines were abandoned, and with them, the ability to create many fine movements. While most of the focus in this decade was on the quartz watch, by the mid-1970s Switzerland was regaining its strength and recovering lost ground so that by the end of that decade the country once again had a firm hold on the mechanical watch market. Fine Swiss watches of the 1970s typically went in one of two different design directions: elegant or fashion-forward. Many high-fashion cuff watches of open-worked metal appeared during this time, as did watches that were sleek and stark in design. Asymmetrical watches and odd-shaped bracelet links appeared on the scene, as perfect accents for the expanding ready-to-wear market. For men, elegance returned in the form of bracelet watches with clean lines and understated, integrated case-to-bracelet-to-dial designs.

TOP From A. Lange & Söhne, "The Little 1" features a manually wound, patented movement with outsized date, power reserve indicated, stop seconds and twin barrels for three-day power reserve.

ABOVE The 1990s saw a rise in watches with calendar features. This Torus from Parmigiani Fleurier has an automatic movement with calendar.

TOP RIGHT This elegant minute repeater wristwatch from Parmigiani Fleurier is crafted in 18K white gold with a stepped bezel.

RIGHT Bedat & Co's No. 7 curved rectangular wristwatch features an automatic movement and classic styling.

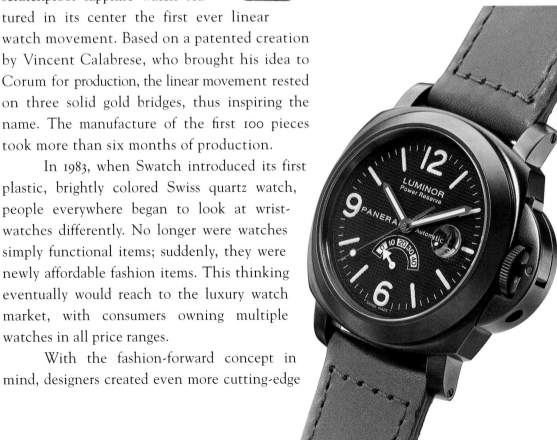

The 1980s was a decade of interesting developments in wristwatches. Computer-aided design became more and more important, and novel types of wristwatches appeared on the market. Watch manufacturers turned more attention to the use of new and different materials for wristwatches during this decade, including rubber for straps and titanium and ceramic for bracelets and cases.

Additionally, having introduced high-tech, avant-garde and unusual-shaped wristwatches, the Swiss watch industry turned once again to creating wonderful jeweled pieces, further miniaturizing movements, perfecting chronographs and creating complicated movements for use in wristwatches.

In 1980, after three years of development and fine-tuning, Corum introduced the Golden Bridge watch. A technical revolution at the time, the entirely transparent scratchproof sapphire watch featured in its center the first ever linear watch movement. Based on a patented creation by Vincent Calabrese, who brought his idea to Corum for production, the linear movement rested on three solid gold bridges, thus inspiring the name. The manufacture of the first 100 pieces took more than six months of production.

In 1983, when Swatch introduced its first plastic, brightly colored Swiss quartz watch, people everywhere began to look at wristwatches differently. No longer were watches simply functional items; suddenly, they were newly affordable fashion items. This thinking eventually would reach to the luxury watch market, with consumers owning multiple watches in all price ranges.

With the fashion-forward concept in mind, designers created even more cutting-edge

BELOW Recalling the longest American space mission, the Omega Speedmaster Professional Skylab 3 watch features the official mission patch at 9.

CENTER OVAL Franck Muller's World Wide Collection pays homage to the five continents with a different continent on each dial, accompanied by a compass card. The model shown is World Wide Asia featuring a dual time zone, crafted in 18K rose gold.

BELOW Patek Philippe's Quantieme Annual wristwatch is an automatic calendar watch that indicates date, day, month and moon phase.

wristwatch designs, with integrated bracelets and cases, cuff watches, and even asymmetrical and horseshoe-shaped cases. High-jeweled creations began to flourish as well as many jewelry and watch houses, such as Cartier, Chopard and Piaget, began adorning women's watches with diamonds and gemstones from end to end.

In 1988, Movado began its Artists' Watch series. Each year the company would introduce a limited edition wristwatch created by a particular artist. The first, in 1988, called the Times/5 featured five different Andy Warhol snapshots of New York City. Only 250 wristwatches were created shortly after Warhol's death. The 1989 artist was Yaacov Agam, whose Rainbow collection of watches featured very colorful yet minimalistic designs.

The transition from the 1980s to the 1990s did not produce drastic changes in the direction of watch design. However, with more fast-paced, hectic business schedules, increased air travel and worldwide banking and interfacing, significant strides were made in improving wristwatch functions. Master watchmakers are producing even their finest watch models with chronograph functions, often with alarms, pulsimeters and other measurement devices built in. Chronometers, too, are almost a staple for many of the fine watchmaking houses. It seems consumers are more eager to purchase a product that has a certificate affirming that the watch has been tested and approved under the most stringent of circumstances.

Also during the past decade, highly advanced complicated wristwatches have carved a new niche. Girard-Perregaux, for instance, reconceptualized and miniaturized its nine-

teenth-century Tourbillon with three gold Bridges pocket watch to fit the movement into a wristwatch. The company has, every year since, introduced a magnificent new Tourbillon with three gold Bridges wristwatch. IWC achieved a horological accomplishment in the 1990s: one of the world's most complex wristwatch movements. The 11 Destriero Scafusia, fondly nick-named the "warhorse," has a total of twenty-one different functions and displays, including a tourbillon, perpetual calendar, chronograph with flyback hand, minute repeaters and moon phase. Its movement consists of 750 individual parts. Audemars Piguet introduced the Grande Complication, whose movement consists of more than 400 parts. The watch features minute repeater, split-second chronograph, perpetual calendar with moon phase and is ensconced in diamonds.

*S*everal important new brands producing mechanical and complicated wristwatches have emerged in the 1990s, as well. Franck Muller came on the scene with a plethora of complicated timepieces under his own name. Blancpain opened its doors with the very complicated 1735 (tourbillon, minute repeater, perpetual calendar) platinum wristwatch, and a myriad of other mechanical wristwatch products.

In 1998, several fine watch companies focused attention on multiple time zone wristwatches, GMT timepieces and updated calendar

TOP RIGHT Blancpain's Chronograph with Flyback hand is at once clean, sophisticated and inspiring.

ABOVE The Rolex Oyster Perpetual Day-Date wristwatch is a newer version of its water-resistant namesake, which made headlines in the 1920s.

LEFT Hamilton's Chronograph Automatic features a day/date counter with chronograph functions.

functions. Patek Philippe, for instance, turned its attention to the self-winding annual calendar wristwatch, introducing a new patented watchmaking complication. The beauty of this function is in its simplicity. On most mechanical annual calendar watches, the wearer needs to reset the date at the end of the months that have fewer than thirty-one days. The Patek Philippe annual calendar watch, which shows the day and the month on the dial, can automatically adjust for months with thirty or thirty-one days, thus requiring just one reset a year, at the end of February. It achieves this by use of an ingenious wheel-based mechanism consisting of two wheel assemblies that determine the date change. Another Patek Philippe patent introduced in 1998 is for its Travel Time wristwatch. This dual-time-zone watch features a design that allows the wearer to "tuck" the second time-zone indicator beneath the first time-zone hand when not in use so that the watch looks like a single-time-zone watch.

*I*n more moderately priced wristwatches, the latter half of the 1990s sees greater attention being paid to "items." Solar powered watches, which had been introduced to the world in small numbers in the 1970s, became more prevalent, with not only the Japanese, but also the Swiss, creating watches powered by sun and natural light. The Swiss watch brand Swatch further pushed technology forward by introducing a series of important breakthroughs in this decade, from the Swatch Solar to the Swatch Musical melodious alarm clock wristwatches. In the lower-end wristwatch category, on the eve of the new millennium, wristwatches are fast being developed that

will have computer link-ups, organizational databases, beepers, pagers and telephones.

While it is difficult to say if luxury watch manufacturers will follow suit on these technological advancements, as the twenty-first century approaches, Swiss watchmakers continue perfecting fine wristwatches, adding functions, complications and calendars that will make significant contributions to watch design in the new millennium.

DAWN OF A NEW ERA

Despite the popularity of mechanical wristwatches, by the first decade of the twentieth century, scientists, mathematicians and engineers were demanding more precise time measurement than could be achieved by conventional devices. In this era of the Wright Brothers and ragtime, the quest began for something that could swing, oscillate, or vibrate faster — and thus dissect time more exactly — than the traditional balance wheel and hairsprings of the mechanical watch. This quest would culminate seventy years later, in the era of the Concorde and disco music, with the introduction of a new standard in precision and convenience for commercial timepieces — the quartz wristwatch. In the 1920s, as telephone and radio broadcasting technology matured, devising better, more efficient electronic

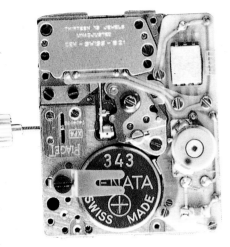

means to monitor frequencies became a technical imperative. Experimenters in the radio and telecommunications fields turned to Pierre Curie's works. Years earlier, near the turn of the century, Curie observed and documented the phenomenon of piezoelectricity. Curie described for the first time how quartz crystals vibrate — changing their shapes slightly, back and forth — when electricity passes through them.

With this fact in mind, scientists and inventors turned increasing attention to quartz crystals. They were found to be effective energy resonators and controllers: if their oscillations could be slowed and steadied, quartz crystals could prove valuable in timekeeping. Building on this theory, in 1927-28, Canadian-born Warren Marrison, seeking more reliable frequency standards while working at Bell Telephone Laboratories in the United States, developed the first quartz clock. The clock's accuracy was lauded and it was judged to provide the most precise time keeping yet developed. Nonetheless, it took nearly a full decade for the concept

A master stroke.

ETERNA

THE TIME COMPUTER

Pulsar

to translate into commercial production. By the 1940s, though, large quartz crystal clocks powered by electricity had become the standard in laboratories and observatories.

Still, no one could envision the use of quartz crystals and electric power in tiny wristwatches. In fact, it was not until two decades later — with the invention of the integrated circuit in 1959 — that the idea of quartz watches became more than just a faint glimmer of hope. The integrated circuit is essentially an electronic circuit reduced photographically onto a semiconductive silicon surface. Savvy scientists and watchmakers recognized the potential of the integrated circuit in watchmaking and jumped on the

invention bandwagon, realizing that the integrated circuit — the equivalent of hundreds of thousands of resistors and transistors in an area one centimeter or less on its side — could act as a conductor within the watch.

Around the same time, Swiss engineer Max Hetzel had invented the tuning fork–controlled watch — in which the balance wheel is replaced by a tiny tuning fork controlled by a small battery and an electronic circuit. He brought his invention to Swiss watchmakers, who brushed off the concept in favor of their beloved mechanical timepieces. Hetzel sold the concept to Bulova, which in 1960 introduced the Accutron watch with tuning fork-control. It was an instant success and the Swiss later found themselves buying rights to use the technology.

the size and shape of the crystals, and the voltage applied. The circuit carries out the functions of the watch, including the electronic counting of the vibrations of the quartz crystal resonator to provide precise time standards. The concept was strong, and many watchmakers around the world, particularly the Swiss and the Japanese, had the foresight to believe in and pursue it.

Taking on the challenge of developing the new technology, the Swiss assigned the project in 1960 to a team at the Centre Electronique Horloger (CEH) research laboratory. Their job was to develop a quartz-controlled, integrated circuit wristwatch. By 1961, they had conceived of and created a prototype of a large, bulky quartz watch that was more precise than any

ABOVE In 1976, Piaget developed the then thinnest quartz movement, the 7P. This white gold cushion-shaped watch with Lapis Lazuli dial uses the 7P movement.

ABOVE RIGHT By the 1980s, Swiss watch manufacturers began adorning quartz movement watches with gemstones and diamonds. This 1982 Piaget bracelet watch features alternating rows of 264 diamonds and 144 sapphires.

RIGHT Launched by Girard-Perregaux in 1976, this unusual wristwatch features an LED digital display.

With a hard lesson learned, when the concept of quartz crystal power for wristwatches emerged, the Swiss watch industry collectively decided to pursue the research.

A quartz watch — in its original concept and still today — essentially consists of an integrated circuit, a battery and a quartz crystal oscillator, which is made to vibrate by the energy supplied by the battery. The frequency of the quartz vibrations depends on

mechanical counterpart. However, the new technology required weekly battery changes. The CEH continued its quest and by 1967 had produced a somewhat smaller, thinner quartz crystal watch. The first manufactured product, the Beta 21, was developed and produced in 1969 and was to be made commercially available in April 1970.

However, the reliability of the quartz time-pieces (far greater than that of any mechanical watch) frightened the Swiss watch industry, which worried that its tradition of craftsmanship might be overthrown by this new technology. About the same time, the Japanese announced that they were close to the development of production-line manufactured quartz timepieces, and the Swiss did not have the industrial capacity to

ABOVE In 1979, Longines introduced its ultra-flat quartz watch, called the Gold Leaf, with the newest flat movement of the time, comparing its thinness to a match stick.

BELOW LEFT The introduction of the Swatch Watch in 1983 helped to revive the Swiss watch industry, and turned watches into fashion accessories with its affordability and design. These Folon Swatches were introduced in the 1980s,

compete on that level. Furthermore, believing that quartz was a craze and the public would never lose its desire for and love of fine mechanical wristwatches for what many traditionalists regarded as cheap imitations, the Swiss watch industry as a whole backed off from aggressive marketing of quartz technology.

Despite its head start, the Swiss watch industry failed to see the enormous potential of the quartz watch and collectively dropped the pursuit to be among the leaders — a mistake that would cost them dearly. In 1970, only sixteen Swiss watch companies began using the Beta 21 quartz movements under their own brand names in products that would appear on the market a year or so later. The Swiss and the Japanese were both working on the quartz project at about the same time and were neck and neck in technologi-

cal development. Despite the fact that the Swiss had mastered the technology, they abandoned the effort to bring it to market first, giving the battle up to the Japanese. To this day, many argue over who really created the first quartz watch, but there is no argument over who first produced and marketed a commercial line of such watches.

It was the Japanese who first came to market fully with an analog quartz watch, edging out the Swiss and the Americans by just a few months. The Japanese, much like the Swiss, had been quick to pursue the concept of quartz watches. As early as 1959, Seiko had put together a team of researchers whose objectives were to produce a quartz watch at reasonable prices through volume production. In late 1963, they had developed quartz crystal, battery-powered chronometers,

BELOW LEFT This Movado watch is part of the Safiro collection and features the signature Museum dial in sapphire blue.

BELOW The women's limited edition watches from Hublot use quartz movements. These are two recently introduced pieces. The Falcon features an entirely enameled dial, while Wild Horses features a low-relief engraving technique on its dial.

brand was developing a line of quartz crystal watches that were accurate to within five seconds a month, or a minute a year — retailing for about $1,250.

In April of 1970, just months after Seiko's introduction of the SQ Astron analog quartz watch, American firm Hamilton Watch Company announced the introduction of the world's first solid state digital quartz crystal wristwatch prototype, called the Pulsar. The Pulsar utilized LED (light-emitting diode) technology that had first been developed in 1962 for other industries. It had a digital readout that indicated the time of day in bright red digits that lit up with the push of a button. This significant advance in watchmaking was the result of a joint effort in research and design by Hamilton Watch Company and Electro/Data, Inc.

The first Hamilton Pulsar wristwatches were marketed as space-age technology and immediately became the rage: the Pulsar was soon in hot demand by celebrities, senators, shahs and emperors around the world. In 18-karat gold, it sold for about $2,100. In 1972, Hamilton

one of which was used in the Olympic Games in Tokyo in 1964. On Christmas day in 1969, Seiko introduced its first line of quartz crystal analog wristwatches, the SQ Astron, in a limited production of 100 pieces. By 1971 and into 1972, the

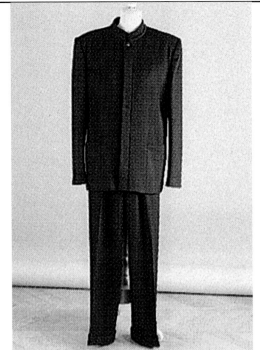

was producing more than 1,000 Pulsars a week, and was still in a "sold-out" capacity four months in advance. Within a year, the company was producing 14-karat-gold-filled versions for $1,275 and stainless steel for $275.

These very first quartz watches had several inherent problems, however. They were prohibitively expensive (often costing more than a thousand dollars) because of the initial cost of the technology. In addition, because the crystal and circuit technology was still in its infancy, these watches were large, cumbersome and generally unattractive. Battery life was short, sometimes just a few months, and the initial technology was not user-friendly. The LED technology utilized in these early digital watches required the user to press a button to see the readout of time on the watch face. While at first these digital wristwatches were very popular, consumers later began to complain about the inconvenience of having to push a button to display the time — and this first genera-

tion of digital watches soon fell out of favor.

Once again the world's ever vigilant watchmakers renewed their efforts to improve on existing technology. Over time, the Japanese had extended watch battery life to years instead of months. Some companies were also working on creating slimmer movements and more attractive designs. Quartz watches from companies such as Seiko and Citizen began to appear with calendars, chronographs and other functions. Watchmakers replaced the unpopular LED watches with LCD (liquid crystal display) technology. Whereas LED watches lit only when the wearer pushed a button, LCD watches maintained a constant readout.

While the American watch market had been in a slump prior to the early 1970s, this introduc-

tion of technology breathed new, albeit temporary, life into American's watch industry. Not only did American watch companies jump on board the digital quartz revolution, so did companies in other industries. American firms, such as Texas Instruments, Fairchild and Gillette, which had access to integrated circuits were grabbing them up and having them cased into inexpensive digital quartz timepieces in Asian countries where labor was cheap.

Within a year, low-end digital quartz crystal watches began flooding the market. In short order, average watch prices plunged from several hundred dollars to as little as $10. Consumers were snapping up these timepieces almost faster than the companies could produce them. Still, the market for these inexpensive items would be short-lived. Japan, with its low-cost labor and high technology, began to reign supreme in the quartz watch business — slowly pushing out the Americans and pulling ahead of the Swiss in terms of units produced.

TOP RIGHT Concord's Impresario Quartz watch for gents features a mother-of-pearl dial.

BOTTOM LEFT These Style de Chaumet watches feature rectangular cases in either steel or 18K gold.

*T*his was the decade that changed world watchmaking production and export patterns forever. In the 1970s, Japanese sales of quartz watches increased tenfold, growing from $2 million to nearly $20 million. While Switzerland was employing much of its expertise to improve and further refine its mechanical watchmaking techniques during this period, its sales could not keep pace. In the decade from 1970 to 1980, as Japanese watch production and exports skyrocketed, Swiss production and exports of

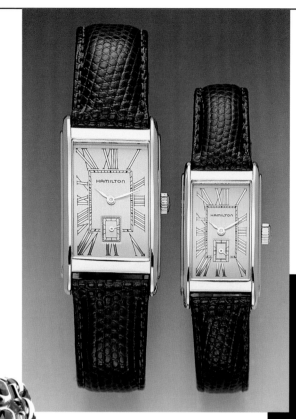

RIGHT The Ardmore, by Hamilton, is based on a 1934 design. It features precision quartz movements and comes in two sizes.

FAR RIGHT From the No. 3 series in the BEDAT & CO. watch line, this elegant quartz analog timepiece features a mesh bracelet and a diamond bezel in an unusual tonneau-styled case.

CENTER RIGHT The Laureato Lady by Girard-Perregaux is enriched with baguette- or brilliant- cut diamonds for timeless elegance.

BELOW This sapphire adorned watch is from the Boutique collection by Daniel Roth.

watches waned. Smaller companies closed their doors, consolidation took hold and the Swiss watch industry suffered major sales declines and a massive number of bankruptcies and closures.

Still, some Swiss watch companies began to embrace the quartz technological revolution in the mid-1970s, slowly introducing quartz watches into their lines while continuing to produce their mechanical masterpieces. In fact, in the first two years of the decade, firms such as Patek Philippe, Piaget, Girard-Perregaux and Eterna had already introduced quartz watch- es into their lines. Patek Philippe, for instance, presented wristwatches with the Beta 21 movement in April of 1970, and then made a concerted effort to develop its own quartz calibers (movements) with analog time displays.

Girard-Perregaux's quartz watch marked the start of the company's modern manufacturing era. The brand's first quartz watch, designed in 1970 and produced by the brand in 1971, was cased in an 18-karat white gold round cushioned case. The dial was midnight blue with the design of the integrated circuit on its dial in light blue and red. The watch featured the date at 3 o'clock position and analog minute, hour and second hands. Two years later, in 1973, Girard-Perregaux introduced a revolutionary looking LED digital quartz watch with a streamlined case in a strikingly avant-garde, definitively ahead-of-its-time design.

Longines also moved ahead on the quartz project and in 1972 was awarded the American IR 100 prize for its first quartz LCD wristwatch.

In 1975, Heuer introduced the first quartz wrist chronograph: the Chronosplit. The digital timepiece had a liquid crystal display, two batteries and what was considered a thin case at the time. For the next several years, the firm perfected its sport quartz wristwatches. Similarly, in 1975, Breitling's offerings inclu- ded a quartz version of the Chronomat and, later, quartz versions of the Navitimer and other popular models.

Piaget took a differ-ent tack from the start, introduc-ing jeweled wristwatches with unusual case shapes and elegant bracelets. Among Piaget's original collections of quartz wristwatches was a series of cuff watches, presented in the early 1970s, that boasted wide dials and elaborate bracelets. In 1976, Piaget presented the 7P movement, at that point the thinnest quartz movement in the world, to offer a variety of high-jewelry, diamond-and-precious-stone ladies' wristwatches. Piaget also used the 7P movement in its Polo line, which was created during this period.

All of those firms that produced quartz watches did so with vim and vigor in terms of design. The 1970s represented a lively spirit; tech-

ABOVE LEFT Baume & Mercier's Catwalk is an elegant bracelet watch with the dial integrated right into the bracelet design.

ABOVE The 1752QZ Cintree Curvex from Franck Muller is cased in 18k white gold and is water resistant to 30 meters.

LEFT Corum's Tobogan Racing watch is striking in bright red. Available either with a quartz or automatic movement, this watch has an ingenious design that allows the wearer to transform it into a mini table clock.

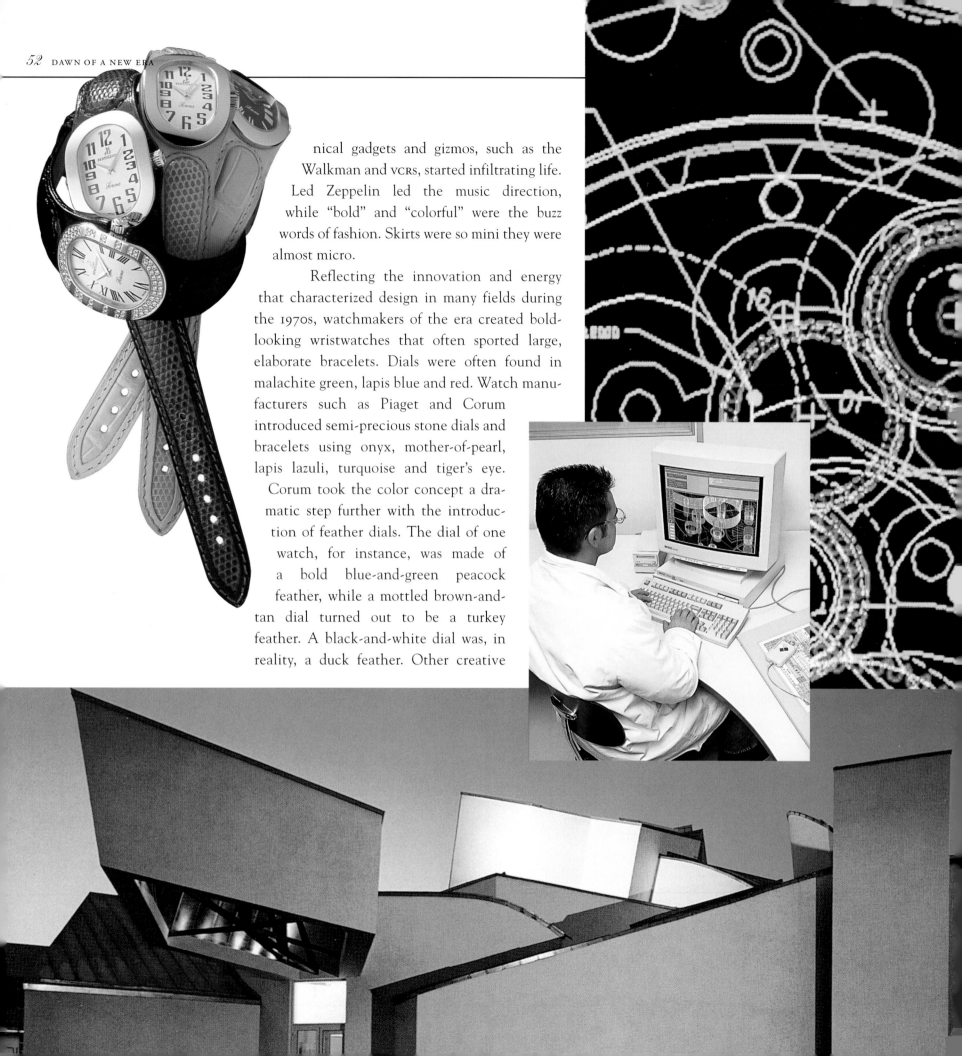

nical gadgets and gizmos, such as the Walkman and VCRs, started infiltrating life. Led Zeppelin led the music direction, while "bold" and "colorful" were the buzz words of fashion. Skirts were so mini they were almost micro.

Reflecting the innovation and energy that characterized design in many fields during the 1970s, watchmakers of the era created bold-looking wristwatches that often sported large, elaborate bracelets. Dials were often found in malachite green, lapis blue and red. Watch manufacturers such as Piaget and Corum introduced semi-precious stone dials and bracelets using onyx, mother-of-pearl, lapis lazuli, turquoise and tiger's eye.

Corum took the color concept a dramatic step further with the introduction of feather dials. The dial of one watch, for instance, was made of a bold blue-and-green peacock feather, while a mottled brown-and-tan dial turned out to be a turkey feather. A black-and-white dial was, in reality, a duck feather. Other creative

Swiss watch companies also turned to different materials such as stones and multi-colored enameling to add color and life to their watches during this era.

$\mathscr{B}$y the late 1970s, recognizing the profitability of quartz watches, the Swiss watch industry collectively agreed on the need to fully join in the quartz revolution. Quartz was not a fad — it was a definitive advance in precise timing and could not be ignored. Swiss watchmakers now had to climb out of their crises and produce quartz watches in greater quantities. The Swiss fought to regain their advantage by concentrating on multi-readout and analog readout styles. Whereas the Japanese had mastered the production of digital quartz watches, the strength of the Swiss was in their beautiful dials, wheel trains and hands. They pursued the production of quartz analog wristwatches, and — rather than purchase Japanese movements — the Swiss watch industry created its own movements (partnering when necessary with technology firms to develop its own integrated circuits) that could be sold to other watch companies around the world — furthering

the eventual recovery of the Swiss watch industry.

Once on board the quartz bandwagon, the Swiss delved into further perfecting the quartz watch — looking to make it slimmer, dressier, more precise. With Japan's Citizen Watch Company having set a record with a 1-mm-thick quartz movement that was 4-mm thick when set in the case, the Swiss firm ETA (owned by ASUAG, Allgemeine Schweizererische Uhrenindustrie AG) set out to beat that record. In 1979 ASUAG, Concord, Eterna and Longines, which had been working together, introduced the world's flattest quartz wristwatch with analog indication. Including the case, it was less than 2mm thin (1.98mm, to be exact). It was sold initially by each company involved: as the Concord Delirium, the Eterna Espada and the Longines Gold Leaf. From there, even thinner movements were developed — enabling Switzerland once again to prove its technical prowess.

Another significant boost to the recovery of Switzerland's watch business came from what would become one of the most popular, affordably priced watch brands ever produced by a Swiss firm. Utilizing the quartz analog technology and radically reinterpreting the concept of fashion in watchmaking, in 1983, Swiss watch giant ASUAG/SSIH (today known as

Swatch Group Ltd.) intro- duced a revolutionary product: the Swatch watch.

Three years in design and development, Swatch not only drew worldwide attention to Switzerland's watchmaking once again, but also revolutionized consumers' attitudes about watches — making them fashion statements rather than simply functional items.

Created as a fun fashion watch crafted in plastic and base metal, Swatch would rattle the Swiss watch industry with its retail price of $35. The novel concept of the Swatch watch technology is its design, in which the base of the metal watch case holds the mountings of the components, so that the electronic module is riveted directly onto the base back. The dial, hands and disk showing the day of the week are then mounted onto this and the entire case is sealed with the plastic crystal in a watertight seal. Whereas most quartz analog watches consist of ninety-nine parts, the Swatch has only fifty-one parts and, because the watch is mounted from the top, production costs are lower. The battery, which is the only replaceable part in the watch, is mounted on the case back.

On March 1, 1983, the first spring/summer Swatch collection was unveiled in seven different countries. By January 20, 1994, Swatch had already sold one million watches. Swatch was the first company to promote the idea of fashion watches as accessories to clothing, and it ushered in a new era of appreciation of wristwatches.

By 1984, watches were no longer considered simply as timepieces, but rather as lifestyle statements. Watch sales soared, particularly in the United States. In fact, in the two years from 1984 to 1986, US watch sales at retail increased more than 28 percent. The average American, who had owned one watch, is now estimated to own three or four watches.

Swatch ushered in a resurgence of interest in analog watches over digital. By 1986, consumer interest had shifted considerably away from digital displays (except for use in sporty timepieces, or as lower-end casual watches) to the more traditional analog dial. Of all watches sold in 1986 in the United States, approximately 65 percent were

quartz analog. Despite the popularity of bright, colorful Swatch watches, the majority of the fine wristwatches of this decade were toned down quite a bit from the styles of the 1970s. They were simpler, cleaner in line and design and offered a quieter statement, reflecting the more sober attitude in society that was taking hold. Computers were invading the business world, high-technology was entering the homes and there was a renewed respect for classicism taking hold in society.

The perfecting of quartz technology during this time made possible anatomically curved quartz timepieces and extremely precise wristwatches. The crystals inside today's watches vibrate anywhere from about 33,000 to 4 million times per second, providing the most precise time standard available next to the atomic clock.

By the late 1980s, the global quartz watch

ABOVE LEFT From Omega, the Constellation watch offers sporty elegance.

ABOVE CENTER The tonneau-shaped Allegro from Raymond Weil features a date window at 6.

ABOVE From the Tesoro collection by Tiffany, these timepieces offer simple, classic elegance.

CENTER OVAL This unusual egg-shaped timepiece from Mellerio Meller features diamonds and heart-shaped sapphires for overall elegance.

industry had settled into its currently recognizable form. American production was basically nonexistent, due to buyouts by foreign companies. Bulova and a few other companies remained intact and continued to offer quartz timepieces, primarily manufacturing them overseas. The Japanese were known for moderately priced gold-plated fashionable watches that sported thin cases in square or round designs and matching bracelets. Hong Kong had largely taken over the production of low-end plastic timepieces.

The Swiss, producing both sport and dress watches, had a firm hold on the middle- to upper-priced quartz business. By 1986, for instance, Patek Philippe was producing 34 percent of its line with quartz movements. One of the strongest markets for Swiss quartz watches was women. Women preferred quartz to mechanical watches, it was believed, because the quartz watch did not have to be set and reset constantly, and because the thinness of the movement generally meant a more attractive case design. In addition, Switzerland was the only country that

could successfully introduce and sell extremely elaborate quartz watches in 18-karat gold and diamonds — thanks once again to the country's illustrious watchmaking heritage.

The 1990s saw the introduction of a great variety of quartz wristwatches from the finest manufacturers who had now recognized their potential. Still careful to preserve their dedication to mechanical watchmaking, these watchmakers utilized quartz for freedom in design.

In October, 1992, Piaget introduced a complex quartz analog movement, caliber 212P, producing the smallest chronograph with flyback function and perpetual calendar. It was created by Piaget in collaboration with Cartier and Baume & Mercier. Piaget used this movement in its Protocole Redonde, Tanagra and Dancer watches.

In 1994, master watchmaker Franck Muller introduced quartz movements to his collection in the mini-curved Cintrée Curvex line, and has expanded quartz to many of his women's watch models, offering a choice of either quartz or mechan-

FAR LEFT The Fantasy by Van Cleef & Arpels offers the unusual feature of a simple interchangeable bracelet or strap design.

LEFT The Trinity from Cartier features modern style and color. The intertwining bands of pink, white and yellow gold in the watch case offer elegance and versatility. It houses a Cartier quartz movement.

ical movements. In 1996, Patek Philippe introduced the Neptune collection of water-resistant sport wristwatches, the women's version of which was fitted with a quartz movement. Today, the majority of Patek Philippe's women's watches in the Gondolo, Ellipse, Flame and Neptune collections are quartz timepieces. Also in the 1990s, Longines introduced its Le Grande Classique col-lection of quartz wristwatches that are just 1.4 millimeters in diameter with classically elegant design.

Along with these elegant 18-karat gold and diamond watches, many other quartz watches also show a high degree of individuality and personality. Today's fine quartz watches run the gamut from high-jeweled masterpieces, to classically elegant bracelet watches, to bright, colorful strap watches, to timepieces with sportier appeal. The quartz revolution had paved new roads in every field of wristwatch design.

AFTER EIGHT

*A*t every ball, black-tie soiree, or gala event, women outdo each other with diamonds and gemstones dripping from head to foot. Tiaras, necklaces, bracelets, earrings and rings make a special statement of stature, beauty, elegance and taste. But as one holds the champagne flute, or martini glass, gestures with a wave of the hand or a cunning, sensual move of the arm — it is the jewels on the wrist that hold eye-catching prominence. With this in mind, watch manufacturers over the decades have sought to combine their functional craft with tantalizing artistry to create high-jeweled watches that take one's breath away. Few things in life are as beautiful or entrancing as diamonds and gemstones. These treasures of the earth have been leaving their mark on mankind ever since their discovery. For centuries,

precious stones have been the objects of desire for royalty around the world. Used as icons of power, strength, healing, mystery, love and passion, the allure of these stones runs deep. With a variety that echoes nature's inherent richness, gemstones offer unparalleled bursts of color and profound beauty. Found in every imaginable hue — each one unique — rich red rubies, entrancing green emeralds, stunning blue sapphires and sparkling diamonds are the rarest and most beautiful stones in the world.

The use of colored stones in jewelry can be traced back to the third century BC. Since then, jewelers and great jewelry-making houses have been obsessed with using these wonders in their creations. Using them in the art of watchmaking, though, is a relatively new phenomenon. Of course, watches themselves are also a recent development, claiming but a few centuries of history.

The first known portable watches to flaunt gemstones can be traced back to the sixteenth century, when Calvinism banned the wearing of jewelry — though not watches — and jewelers and watchmakers joined efforts to create jeweled watches. Early high-jeweled portable watches were predominantly

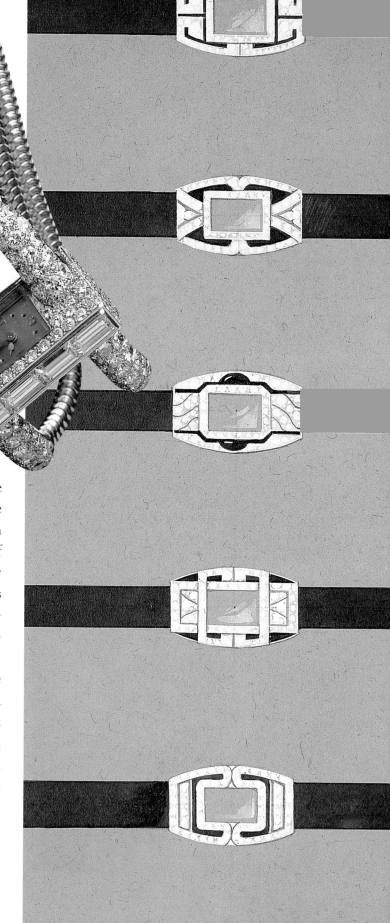

made to order and were specially set with royalty in mind. It was in the 1800s that the first token wristwatches began appearing on the scene, but they were simple timepieces, not adorned with gemstones.

It was not until the early 1900s that wristwatches began appearing more prominently on the scene, and it was a decade or so past the turn of the century before they truly became the watches of choice. By the early 1920s, with the advent of wristwatches as the twentieth-century preference, great watchmaking houses began paying much more attention to the use of gemstones as accents.

*D*uring the next-decade-and-a-half, socializing became an increasingly popular pastime. From the mid 1920s to the early 1940s, was an extraordinary time, when poets, musicians, fashion designers and writers met at wonderful galas and intimate dinners. They wore the best cloth-

ABOVE This Vacheron Constantin timepiece, circa 1952, offers a mesh bracelet whose ornate design mimics a belt and buckle.

LEFT These Audemars Piguet Charleston watches deftly recall the art deco period.

FAR LEFT In this Boucheron ladies' wristwatch from 1890, "Paris street-boys" play among foliated scrolls.

BELOW In the 1920s, many of the great jewelry houses created art deco designs to appeal to women. Shown here are some Van Cleef & Arpels watches, circa 1924 and 1925.

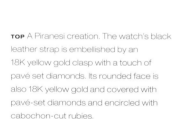

ing, the most fashionable jewelry and the newest timepieces. During this period, high-jeweled watchmaking boomed. Art nouveau and art deco wristwatches dominated the scene, often sporting diamonds with onyx, lapis lazuli, malachite, mother of pearl, pearls or other stones. Most of these were elaborate pieces of jewelry rather than simply functional timepieces, created in an effort to make wristwatches more appealing to discriminating women.

This trend toward opulent wristwatches was interrupted by the onset of World War II. But in the post-war decades of the 1950s and 1960s, as fashion designers inspired new looks for women, once again "dressing to the nines" for After Eight hours became a way of life, and once again, jeweled watches were in vogue. Watch houses began offering designs that sported precious gemstone bezels in floral or geometric designs. The great houses of Van Cleef & Arpels, Boucheron, Cartier, and Piaget all developed stunning watches setting these stones in petal and leaf patterns.

By the 1970s, gemstones of all types were being used by top watchmakers to create fashionable, luxurious works of art. High-jeweled watches of the 1970s were dramatically styled, referencing the high fashions of the time. Watches

TOP A Piranesi creation. The watch's black leather strap is embellished by an 18K yellow gold clasp with a touch of pavé set diamonds. Its rounded face is also 18K yellow gold and covered with pavé-set diamonds and encircled with cabochon-cut rubies.

ABOVE Nobility is on the minds of Breguet's designers, as is evidenced by this jeweled masterpiece.

RIGHT Created in 1938, this Van Cleef & Arpels "Tourniquet" timepiece is a cuff watch that features diamonds and rubies set on a taut bracelet of supple hexagon links.

FACING PAGE Concord's Saratoga signature timepieces take on a new look bedecked in diamonds and rubies.

were designed with unusual, ultra-modern case shapes. Asymmetrical designs appeared as did square-shaped cases, cuff watches and bolder and stronger looks that juxtaposed semiprecious stone dials and diamond bezels. On the more feminine side, pearls and semiprecious stones were the items of choice for jeweled bracelets.

As watchmakers developed their technical prowess, slimmer movements appeared on the scene, encouraging the introduction of a whole variety of designs in women's watches. By the

1980s, the fashion-forward look gave way to a more traditional sense of luxury, as watchmakers returned to grace, flowing elegance and femininity. The style in cases, which had recently tended to the square and rectangular, now leaned to the oval, round and heart-shape where semiprecious had often appeared, now even more valuable gems were used and diamonds became increasingly prevalent on bracelets, cases and dials in addition to bezels.

The 1980s trend toward elegance further evolved and matured so that the 1990s were ushered in with a new subtlety in high-jewelry time-

pieces. Luxurious designs that bespoke refinement, taste and exquisiteness became the standard in haute joaillerie. Many great houses introduced designs that reflected nature, including flora and fauna, while others focused on making the gemstones themselves the center of attention.

Today, jeweled wristwatches are in a league of their own. Some utilize just a few accent stones; others, innumerable stones that fully encrust the timepiece. While some watchmakers dabble with citrine, amethyst, and a few other semiprecious stones, it is the most precious stones in the world — rubies, emeralds, sapphires and diamonds — that they most often turn to.

The magnificent art involved in bringing together these shimmering gems of the earth with the technial demands of master watchmaking yields some of the most stunning, one-of-a-kind watches in the world. Much like the fine art of watchmaking, the art of selecting and cutting such fine stones is a time-consuming, painstaking process that can take as long, if not longer, than the creation of the timepiece itself. Often the gem cutters and stone setters work in concert with one another to assure the finest match in stones. Most of these grand creations

OPPOSITE PAGE, LEFT Rudolph Valentino and Gloria Swanson wearing Cartier watches and jewelry. **CENTER** Fifth Avenue collection by Harry Winston, named after the glamor of New York city's famous street. These timepieces are offered in diamonds, rubies or sapphires for shimmering delight. **OVAL** This ladies' Curvex case from Franck Muller is set with sapphires and brilliant- and baguette-cut diamonds. It is an exquisite combination of yesterday and today.

ABOVE LEFT Composed of nearly fifty carats of gemstones, this Cartier Parrot, with its diamond feathers, shimmers in elegance each time its head rises to reveal the watch dial.

BELOW Focusing on the floral theme, Audemars Piguet bedecks its stunning white beauty with a flowered diamond case design.

RIGHT Omega's Berenices timepiece, named after the wife of Egyptian King Ptolemy, is characterized by square-cut diamond hour markers (or ruby or sapphire) on a mother-of-pearl dial.

FAR RIGHT The La Scala Diva collection of square wristwatches from Concord comes in a variety of diamond-adorned dials, cases, bezels and bracelets for stunning yet understated beauty.

BELOW RIGHT Audemars Piguet introduces the Flocons de neige, a design meant to resemble snowflakes.

CENTER The Manhattan is Harry Winston's first rectangular wristwatch. Created in 18K gold, the watch is elegantly reminiscent of the roaring twenties.

ate the watch. Once this was accomplished, it took more than 300 hours to cut the stones and an almost similar amount of time to set them. Similarly, it took Vacheron Constantin's jewelers more than 6,000 hours to select and set the 118 diamonds that bedeck the sumptuous Kallista watch. One of the world's most expensive and elaborate diamond wristwatches, the Kallista (valued at $9 million) weighs 130 carats. It is not unusual to hear similar stories of feats of skill and perserverance on the part of great watchmaking houses when it comes to the creation of these representations of femininity and elegance.

Often, these haute joaillerie pieces are inspired by a particular stone, or by a particular image from nature or art. Typically the designer starts with an intricate pencil-sketched rendition that is then filled in with color to indicate the appropriate stone placement. This allows the craftsman to determine how many diamonds and gemstones of a particular size and cut will be needed to create the piece.

command hundreds of individual stones, and hundreds of hours of stone setting, as well.

In the instance of Corum's Claudius watch from the Césars Collection, 400 exceptional quality emeralds were acquired to create a gemological masterpiece. It took the company nearly sixty years to collect enough perfectly matched emeralds from deposits in the former USSR to cre-

From there, the design typically proceeds with the construction of the watch bracelet, which, depending on the type of setting of the stones, can follow several different gold-smithing procedures. Almost as important as the stones used on these spectacular wristwatches is the setting technique. Among the most popular gemstone setting used in watchmaking is pavé, in which tiny round stones are placed so closely together it looks as though the surface is paved with them. Another important technique in setting bracelets and bezels is channel setting, in which the stones are neatly lined up next to one another and held in place between two tracks of gold to form a sleek row of stones with no visible metal. Several great houses of jewelry and watchmaking, such as Chopard, Van Cleef & Arpels, Piaget and Cartier have created their own innovative techniques for stone-setting.

Every stone is set by hand by skilled setters who can work at such tedious handwork only a few hours a day. Polishing of the stones is equally difficult, as the polishers, who also do everything by hand, must get into every facet and crevice of every gemstone once it is set into the timepiece. It is not unusual to find that some of the most spectacular high-carated pieces took months or even years to bring to fruition.

Because gemstones are products of the earth, the issue of rarity comes into play. Often only one watch of a given design can be created because of a lack of enough perfectly matched flawless stones. This is especially true in the case of fancy-colored diamond watches. Sometimes, several timepieces can be created. In the case of unusual pieces that do not take as long to assemble and do not require the rarest of stones, the watchmaker can choose to create the jeweled timepiece in a limited edition. Other, less elaborate designs that simply flaunt diamonds or gemstones as decorations are produced in larger numbers.

Most jeweled wristwatches are set in the finest of metals: Platinum and 18-karat yellow, white or pink gold. However, recent technology has enabled the setting of diamonds into steel — yielding a whole new range of possibilities for jeweled timepieces. Those watch manufacturers utilizing steel for their cases and bracelets, however, do so more to have an affordable gemstone product than to offer uniqueness.

While most gemstone-set gold and platinum masterpieces range in price from thousands of dollars to millions of dollars — depending on the stones used, the caratage and

TOP LEFT AND RIGHT The Neptune from Patek Philippe follows a simple bracelet design that is enhanced with diamonds in both of these watches. The dials feature mother-of-pearl inlays and diamonds.

ABOVE The Arlequin watch from Corum is in keeping with the grand tradition of combining forms with craftsmanship. This semi-cylindrical baguette is designed with enamel lozenges and set with nearly three carats of diamonds.

RIGHT Few treasures in life are as stunning as the pearl. In this creation, Piaget combines the pearl and the ruby in heart-shaped and oval designs for the ultimate statement in love, passion and femininity.

Toutes les Œuvres
de MUCHA
sont en Vente
a
"LA PLUME"
31, Rue Bonaparte.

the setting involved — steel-and-diamond pieces can be had for just a few thousand dollars.

While watch companies acknowledge that men enjoy wearing jeweled wristwatches, especially simple ones with diamond or gemstone markers or bezels, in this category of jewelry timepieces it is truly to women that they cater. Thus it is not unusual to see such themes in high-jeweled watches as floral arrangements, fauna and nature motifs, hidden or secret flip-top watches, architectural and "period"-inspired pieces.

Nature is perhaps the most favored motif in high-jewelry watchmaking when watchmakers choose not just to adorn a piece with gemstones, but also to design it in the likeness of something else. Masters of this magnificent reinterpretation of nature include Cartier, whose famed panthers, birds, elephants and other wild animals exude themselves in superb renditions in diamond or gemstone timepieces.

Many floral motifs are equally as impressive in high-jeweled watchmaking. Van Cleef & Arpels, Chopard, Piaget, Bertolucci, Cartier, Audemars Piguet and several other great houses are masters at creating floral timepieces. Poppies, daisies, posies and a wealth of other flowers provide the inspiration for diamond- and gemstone-adorned timepieces. Other important themes in haute joaillerie include art deco direction, architectural inspiration, fluid lines and forms, and geometry, with watchmakers employing a combination of pure, abstract shapes.

Some watchmakers are also experts at creating high-jeweled watches that are either reversible or have flip-top covers. Bulgari has applied this approach to a snake design, whose head lifts to reveal the timepiece; Jaeger-LeCoultre's famous Reverso elegantly flaunts diamonds and gemstones of varying degrees on its different sides; Vacheron Constantin bedecks its shutter watch (which features gold slats that open and close like blinds to reveal the dial) in diamonds; Cartier offers a rich mix of panthers, peacocks and other animals that raise their heads to reveal the watch.

Certain great watchmaking houses with grand histories and centuries of involvement with royalty, such as Breguet, Patek Philippe, Vacheron

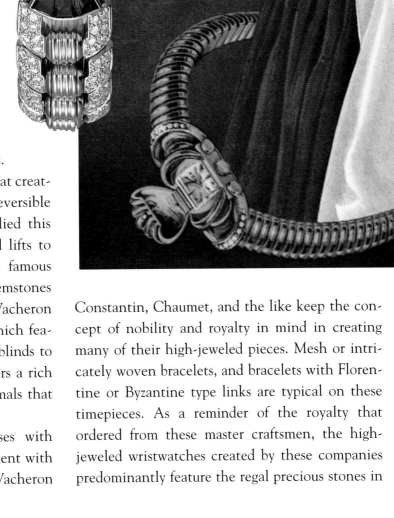

Constantin, Chaumet, and the like keep the concept of nobility and royalty in mind in creating many of their high-jeweled pieces. Mesh or intricately woven bracelets, and bracelets with Florentine or Byzantine type links are typical on these timepieces. As a reminder of the royalty that ordered from these master craftsmen, the high-jeweled wristwatches created by these companies predominantly feature the regal precious stones in

ABOVE LEFT Sapphires and diamonds adorn this Breguet piece combining jewelry and craftsmanship.

ABOVE Omega's artfully inspired 1930s jeweled watch in a rendition reflecting the times.

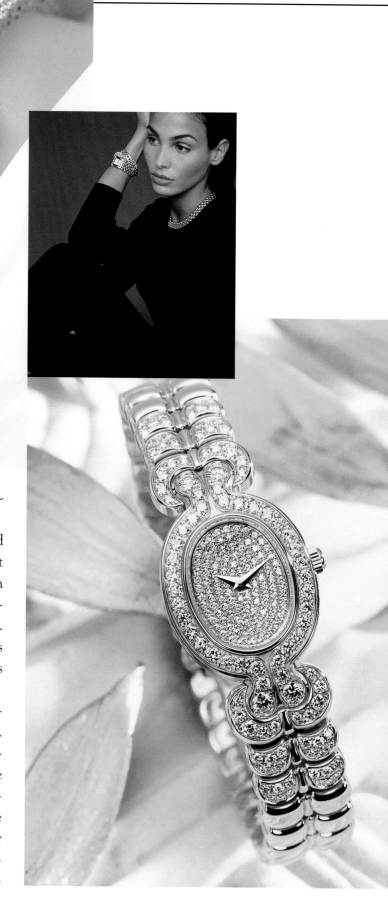

ABOVE OVAL Emerald eyes are always watching in this Cartier masterpiece.

ABOVE CENTER Set with white and yellow diamonds, this Haute Joaillerie Chopard watch in 18K white gold houses nearly 200 diamonds. The stones are cut as marquise, pears and rounds.

ABOVE RIGHT Model wears Chaumet's Khesis collection

RIGHT The Italian Renaissance is a great source of inspiration for watch and jewelry makers. This Vacheron Constantin Les Absolus watch features an oval case and a crescent-link bracelet for soft beauty.

feminine fancy cuts as accent stones in case-to-bracelet attachments or as adornments.

Other companies create their jeweled pieces not to follow a specific motif or theme, but rather to evoke passion and inspire desire with fluid, curvaceous lines. These watches are typically simple, graceful, stunning works of art. Many feature unusual case shapes, such as teardrops, hearts, diamonds, cushioned squares and ovals.

Some companies depend on their own setting techniques to make their watches appealing. Chopard, for instance, perfected its Happy Diamond setting technique that few have been able to mimic. In the Happy Diamond jeweled wristwatches, loose diamonds move freely around the watch above the dial and below the crystal for fluid graceful beauty. Van Cleef & Arpels' invisible settings, in which no gold or platinum is visible, make for breathtaking renditions of pure gemstones. Sarcar's Magic Moon series of timepieces that sport rotating diamond-set motifs, such as horses, sunbursts, golf clubs and an array of different designs in the center of the watch dial make dazzling conversation pieces as well as eye-catching works of art.

No matter the inspiration, one thing is certain: These incomparable works of art represent the pinnacle of craftsmanship and beauty in watchmaking. They are true heirloom items that, as grand as the stones they're made of, will shine for generations to come.

For many, much of the allure of acquiring and wearing a high-jeweled wristwatch stems from the myths and beauty surrounding the regal stones themselves. Often, this is also what attracts the watchmakers to certain stones. Every gemstone, precious or semiprecious, brings with it its own history, mystery, tale of creation and everlasting beauty that holds a different spell over each person attracted to it.

ABOVE Bulgari's intricate Trika timepieces are crafted in 18K white gold and accented with white diamonds.

LEFT Rarely does pink gold shine so brightly as it does in this all-diamond, 18K rose gold Reverso from Jaeger-LeCoultre.

Emeralds, for instance, were long believed to have mystical powers. First unearthed by the Egyptians near the Red Sea almost 4,000 years ago, the emerald was Cleopatra's favorite stone. It was thought that emeralds were able to ward off evil spells and induce clairvoyance, and so were reserved for royalty and great leaders. As a result, the emerald has long been associated with loyalty. Emeralds, also called Venus's

ABOVE With its unusual curved tonneau shaped case set into a manchette-style bracelet, this BEDAT & CO. timepiece is crafted in 18K white gold and offers elegantly subtle beauty.

TOP CENTER This model wears Style de Chaumet watches.

RIGHT Focusing on the alchemy of desire and beauty, Piaget creates this unusual Miss Protocole timepiece that is created in 18K white gold and features diamond case-to-bracelet attachments.

stone, today are considered the symbol of fertility, well-being and good fortune.

The rarest gemstones on earth, emeralds offer a deep, lush green color. They owe their bright green color to small amounts of chromic oxide found in the mineral beryl. Experts agree that the finest stones come from Columbia, but there are also popular sources in Brazil and Zambia. The largest emerald ever unearthed was discovered in 1969 in mines in Gachala, Colombia. It weighed 7,052 carats. Other famous emeralds include a 168-carat rarity that was donated to the Smithsonian Institute in 1931, and two others that passed through the workshops of jeweler extraordinaire Harry Winston. These were the nearly 62-carat Catherine the Great emerald and the 34.40-carat

hexagonal Stotesbury emerald, both of which were sold to private clients.

Emeralds are cut in a variety of shapes, including round, square, oval and the traditional rectangular step-cut that is called "emerald-cut." In timepieces today, round (brilliants), square (carré) and rectangular (baguette) emeralds are most often used.

Another of the rarest and most precious of all gemstones, the ruby offers a deep vibrant red color. The myth of the ruby is that it frees its wearer of cares and worries. Associated with the heart's desire, the ruby is believed to promote a cheerful disposition, to preserve physical and mental health and to give courage to its wearer. Moreover, the ruby is the one gemstone most closely associated with passion and romance.

The ruby owes its red color to the tiny amounts of chromium found in the mineral corundum. Rubies contain thousands of needle-like foreign particles that line up uniformly in the three major directions of atomic structure. Light reflecting from these three sets of needles pro-

duces astersism, a bright starlike reflection that makes the ruby shimmer. The finest quality ruby is even rarer and more valuable than the top quality diamond. Unlike diamonds, though, rubies are difficult to find in large carat weights. In fact, it is rare to see a ruby of more than five carats. One of the most valuable and sizable stones in recent history was a 16-carat ruby that fetched more than a quarter-of-a-million dollars per carat at a 1988 Sotheby's auction.

For more than 500 years the finest rubies have come from a small area called Myanmar, formerly known as Burma, where they are washed from limestone gravels. Rubies also are found in Thailand, Cambodia, Sri Lanka and, to a much smaller extent, North Carolina. Rubies are typically cut in round, oval, square and rectangular-shapes. However, in high-jeweled timepieces rubies often are found cut in fancy shapes, such as pear, teardrop, trapeze or other fancies for use as case-to-bracelet attachment accents. For use on bracelets, rectangular shapes fit neatly, while round cuts are most popular as dial accents.

The sapphire, typically associated with blue, actually comes in a variety of colors, including yellow, orange, pink, lavender and green, though blue remains the most desired. A regal gem, worn by kings for protection, the sapphire is thought to have healing powers and is a symbol of fidelity as well.

Also a form of corundum, sapphires are mostly found in Australia, Thailand, Myanmar and East Africa, with some small quantities found

ABOVE Girard-Perregaux's Chronograph Tourbillon with Three Gold Bridges features mother-of-pearl dial and diamond accents — the ultimate showcase for the highly acclaimed tourbillon movement.

FAR RIGHT Carla Bruni wears Chopard's aptly named Ice Cube watch. It took more than 150 hours to set the 76 square-cut diamonds.

Yellow, champagne, blue, pink and even black diamonds are emerging on the wristwatch scene. It is not unusual to have pink diamonds on an 18-karat pink gold timepiece, white diamonds set in 18-karat white gold or platinum, or yellow diamonds set in 18-karat yellow gold for a total tonal concept. Companies such as Chopard and Cartier have found ways to mix the metals and the fancy-colored diamonds for dazzling appeal. Still, it is the white diamond that gains the most attention from watchmakers.

Regarded as the most important and romantic of gemstones, diamonds were created within the core of the earth more than three billion years ago and brought to the surface by volcanic eruptions. Known since ancient times, diamonds were thought by the Romans to be splinters from falling stars, and by the Greeks to be

in Montana. One of the most magnificent sapphires in history belonged to Catherine the Great. It was a 337-carat sapphire that had also passed through the doors of Harry Winston, who displayed it in a traveling exhibition in the late 1940s and early 1950s. It has since been sold to a private collector.

Sapphires are often used as case and bracelet adornments and in cabochon cuts for the crown of many timepieces because of their hardness. Sapphires are most often found in square, round and rectangular cuts in jeweled wristwatches.

With all of the luster and beauty of the precious colored stones, though, diamonds reign supreme in the watch world. One recent favorite of top watchmakers is natural fancy-colored diamonds.

ABOVE Pastel straps offer new beauty to diamond-and-steel Chaumet timepieces.

LEFT Sheer elegance and beauty sparkle from these teardrop-style Casmir timepieces from Chopard.

tears of the gods. It has long been believed that the diamond is able to give its wearer mystical powers. Today, though, the diamond is most often associated with love and commitment, thanks to the Archduke Maximilian of Austria who in 1477 offered his love, Mary of Burgundy, a diamond engagement ring — beginning a tradition that has become celebrated around the world.

The great house of Harry Winston is, once again, renowned for procuring and selling some of the most famous diamonds of all time, including the Star of Sierra Leone, the Taylor-Burton and the Star of Independence diamonds. The Great

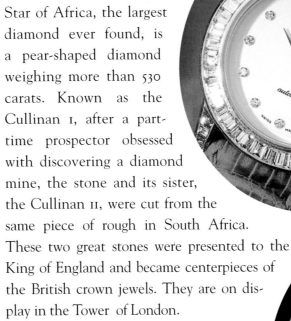

Star of Africa, the largest diamond ever found, is a pear-shaped diamond weighing more than 530 carats. Known as the Cullinan I, after a part-time prospector obsessed with discovering a diamond mine, the stone and its sister, the Cullinan II, were cut from the same piece of rough in South Africa. These two great stones were presented to the King of England and became centerpieces of the British crown jewels. They are on display in the Tower of London.

*D*iamonds can be cut in a great variety of shapes because of their hardness. One cut used primarily for accent stones is the briolette. A teardrop-shaped cut, the briolette is faceted all the way around to bring out dazzling levels of brightness and beauty. The many other cuts in which diamonds are found include round, oval, pear, marquise, cushion and triangular shapes. The round, square, or rectangular cuts are the ones most often used by watchmakers for dials, bezels and cases, because, when properly set they offer superb, dazzling presentations.

Pearls are another favorite of watchmakers, especially for bracelets. Early in the century many

LEFT Blancpain's 18K gold timepiece features 12 diamond markers on the dial and a bezel set with baguette-cut diamonds for simple elegance.

ABOVE Combining its stunning blue chronograph dial with the brilliance of diamonds, Hublot makes a sporty statement in elegant jewelry wristwatches.

LEFT The heart's true desire. Piaget created these heart-shaped timepieces with diamonds and precious stones accented with silk bracelets.

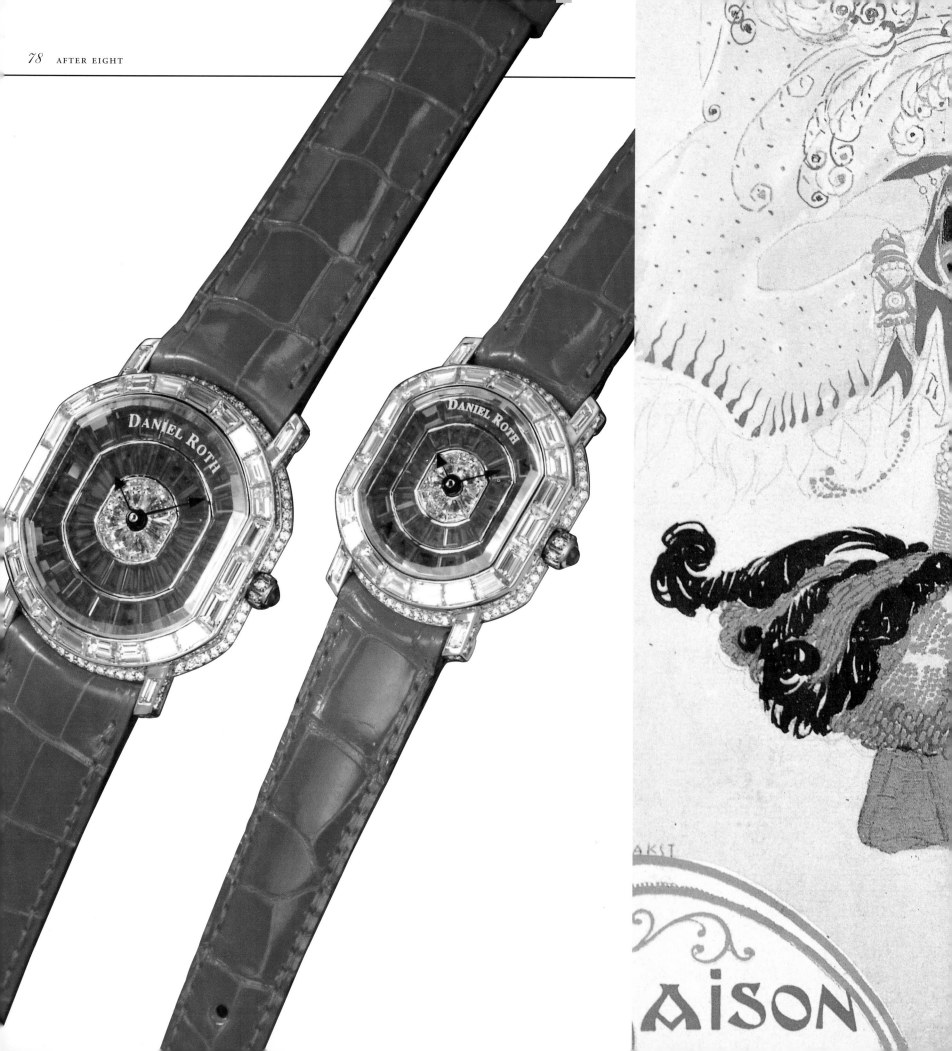

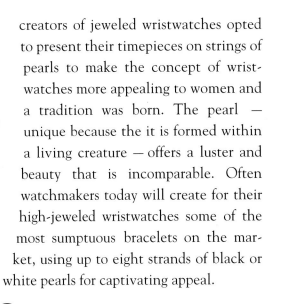

creators of jeweled wristwatches opted to present their timepieces on strings of pearls to make the concept of wristwatches more appealing to women and a tradition was born. The pearl — unique because the it is formed within a living creature — offers a luster and beauty that is incomparable. Often watchmakers today will create for their high-jeweled wristwatches some of the most sumptuous bracelets on the market, using up to eight strands of black or white pearls for captivating appeal.

Emeralds, rubies, sapphires, diamonds and pearls — the hallmarks of high-jewelry watchmaking. The myths and allure that surround these remarkable gemstones guarantee that watchmakers will continue to find new and striking ways to present them. Indeed, the magnificent art of adorning technically masterful timepieces with the world's most beautiful gemstones is one that knows the boundaries only of the great watch designers' minds.

OPPOSITE PAGE Daniel Roth ruby and diamond automatic watches.

ABOVE LEFT Chanel presents a recreation of a timepiece from 1932 in this stunning watch whose bracelet boasts alternating squares of diamonds and onyx.

ABOVE The Semiramis collection of jewelry timepieces from Harry Winsto, crafted in platinum, provides an inspired example of sparking creativity.

LEFT An elegant Piranesi evening watch, beautifully enhanced with repetitive flower motifs with pavé set diamonds in 18K white gold.

WINNING TIME

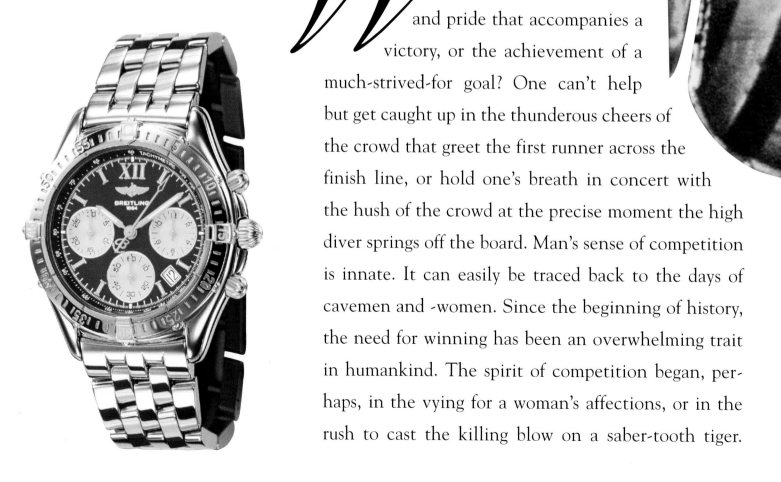

*W*ho can resist the feeling of accomplishment and pride that accompanies a victory, or the achievement of a much-strived-for goal? One can't help but get caught up in the thunderous cheers of the crowd that greet the first runner across the finish line, or hold one's breath in concert with the hush of the crowd at the precise moment the high diver springs off the board. Man's sense of competition is innate. It can easily be traced back to the days of cavemen and -women. Since the beginning of history, the need for winning has been an overwhelming trait in humankind. The spirit of competition began, perhaps, in the vying for a woman's affections, or in the rush to cast the killing blow on a saber-tooth tiger.

OPENING PAGE Breitling's B-One instrument watch features a multifunction electronic movement with analog and digital displays. Among its myriad of functions, it has an alarm, perpetual calendar, chronograph, countdown timer, second time zone with its own alarm and backlit displays.

ABOVE The Admiral's Cup Chrono Fastnet from Corum reflects a conquering spirit. The mechanical chronograph features nautical flags and a succession window to help the sailor maneuver during the first 10 minutes before the race begins.

Over time competitions progressed to staged events between men — such as chariot racing, jousting, archery skills, and the like. Later still, there were dueling matches, fencing matches, horse races and foot races — all in an effort not just to compete, but to win.

As man became more and more civilized, and as the need to win was balanced by a need for ground rules and fair play, the concept of good sportsmanship emerged, helping lead to the modern style of competitive sports pursued for enjoyment. Today we find competition is between men or women, as in foot races, swimming events, tennis matches and other individual or team sports; other times the contest is between man and nature, as is the case with diving, hiking, mountain climbing or skydiving; sometimes the quest has to do with man and machine, as with flying or automobile racing.

In addition to sports activities, there are general races for perfection, or quests to break a record, make a record or do something better or differently than it has been done before. Such quests are manifested in achievements such as

reaching destinations like the South Pole, North Pole, and the top of Mt. Everest, or solo-flying across the Atlantic Ocean, breaking the speed of sound, achieving manned space flights, or walking on the moon. While these are not necessarily sports achievements, feats requiring dependable precision instruments often rely on tough sport timepieces as their wrist equipment because, whether in competitive sports or other forms of achievement, timing is critical. Precise, split-second timing for such events and adventures is a feat that has, over the past century, been honed and refined by the world's finest watchmakers.

The first timing of sports activities in the early 1800s was crude, with measurements made only to the minute. Most often these timekeeping methods involved a series of synchronized stopwatches — hand-held timepieces that were clicked each time the runner (or other type of competitor) made it to the finish line. In 1864, the first short-duration timekeeping that was accurate to within a quarter of a second was made possible. It was the rapidly changing technology of the 1880s and 1890s that spurred further revolutions in timekeeping. Daimler had created its first motor, electricity had been intro-

LEFT The reintroduction in 1997 of the TAG-Heuer Carrera watch saw some updates, including a textured strap and black dial.

BELOW Each of the three watches in the Sea-Earth-Sky Trilogy series from Blancpain offers different features. The GMT is a two-time-zone piece; the Air Command self-winding chronograph with Fly back hand is designed for aviation enthusiasts, and the Fifty Fathoms is a dive watch with unidirectional rotating bezel and is water-resistant to 300 meters. The Fifty Fathoms watch (lower right) is reminiscent of the 1956 Fifty Fathoms that was worn by the divers in Commander Cousteau's film, *The World of Silence.*

RIGHT Breguet's chronograph Rattrapante features a hand wound chronograph movement with fly-back mechanism. It is water-resistant to 30 meters.

BELOW From Harry Winston, the new Indianapolis collection of sport watches features a water-resistant chronograph available in the active colors indicative of sports.

BELOW CENTER These Style De Chaumet 18K gold chronographs offer elegant sports appeal. Featuring mother-of-pearl dials with tritium-treated markers and hands, date indicator and diamonds.

BELOW RIGHT Jaeger-LeCoultre's Master Geographic is a subtly elegant sport timepiece. Housed in a steel case, the timepiece features a second time zone, power reserve and a city disk for 24 time zones. It is water-resistant to 50 meters.

duced, airplanes were flying and watchmakers recognized a need to keep pace and produce precision instruments that would withstand the rigors of a new and changing world.

With perfection in mind, watchmakers progressed in their ability to measure exact time fractions, and introduced measurement to fifths of a second. During the first modern Olympic Games in 1896, American athlete Thomas Burke won the 100-meter dash, finishing one-fifth of a second before Germany's Fritz Hofmann. Watchmakers immediately recognized the need for even more precise timing — watches that could break down the minute to even tinier fractions. Gearing for measurement of tenths of a second, companies such as TAG-Heuer, Breitling, Omega, Movado and

Girard-Perregaux took on the challenge.

In the early 1900s, Breitling had created and patented a stopwatch that had a thirty-minute indicator and a sweep-second hand. Orders for the timepieces came in immediately from police authorities who used them to measure road traffic speeds and, subsequently, to catch speeders.

Indeed, with the technological revolution propelling mankind into the first decades of the new century, not only was time measurement in the forefront of watchmakers' endeavors, but they also began embarking on a quest to fit this precision timing into a wristwatch format. Most organized sports are now timed with elaborate electronic clocks and coordinated computerized cameras. Still, since the turn of the century the sports enthusiast and adventurer enjoy and rely on their wristwatches as their own personal timers. In wristwatches today, the most exact timing — to fractions as minuscule as 1/100th of a second — can come from a sleek chronograph.

*E*ssentially, a chronograph is a timepiece that indicates not only the time of day in hours, minutes and seconds, but is also equipped with an additional mechanism that makes it possible to measure continuous or discontinuous intervals of time, from a fraction of a second up to twelve hours depending on the chronograph. The basic chronograph offers fraction-of-a-second timing to varying degrees depending on the timepiece. Other chronographs, sometimes referred to as Rattrapantes, or Split-Seconds Chronographs, have two second hands, one of which splits, or appears to divide, from the other so that they may act independently of one another. This technology allows the timing of several events which

start at the same time, but have different durations. Some chronographs also have a fly-back hand that automatically returns to zero at the conclusion of timing simultaneous events. There are a wealth of different types of chronographs on the market, and some companies even combine chronograph movements with additional complex watch functions such as calendars, or moon phase functions. Visually, chronographs are almost immediately recog-

ABOVE The Gefica chronograph by Gerald Genta features a mechanical movement with automatic rewind, 1/10th-of-a-second timing and a distinctive case and dial.

LEFT This Pilot Professional Automatic chronograph from Fortis features an alarm. It is fitted with an automatic movement with central rotor and double barrel so the alarm can function without affecting the watch's power reserve or precision.

nizable because of the three small subdials that appear on the chronograph face.

The word chronograph stems from the Greek word *chrono*, meaning time, and the Greek word *graph*, meaning "writer" or "written," producing a literal translation of "time writer." The first such "time writer" was invented by Swiss watchmaker Rieussec in 1822; it was a clock with a hand that was constructed of a small engraving pen that actually wrote the time to be measured on the dial by making a small dot at the beginning of the measuring process and another at the end. The distance between the two dots then represented the time that had passed between them. From there, the ball rolled quickly. Chronographs moved from clocks to pocket watches and finally, with much finessing and perfecting, by the very late 1880s and 1890s, to wristwatches.

By the first decade of the twentieth century, watchmakers had already recognized the usefulness of strong, rugged wristwatches — as witnessed by the military acquisition of such timepieces during the Boer wars of 1899 to 1902. Watch manufacturers made a concerted effort, then, to create even more precise and rugged wristwatch instruments for military and sports uses. Although some watch companies had wrist chronographs by 1912, it was in the mid-1920s that the emergence of the chronograph wristwatch turned into a flood on the market.

The first sport wristwatches in the 1920s were big and rugged looking with large subdials. By the 1930s they were somewhat slimmer and featured clean dial designs, round cases and basic black or

ABOVE In the 1940s watchmakers had progressed to adding a variety of functions to their sport wristwatches. This Breitling Chronomat with slide-rule bezel is circa 1945.

ABOVE RIGHT The Rolex Yacht-Master Superlative Chronometer features a rotating bezel, perpetual automatic movement, screw-down winding crown and Oyster-lock bracelet with safety clasp. It is water-resistant to 100 meters.

RIGHT From the Impressario collection by Concord, these Chronograph and Reserve de Marche timepieces are both rugged certified chronometers.

brown straps. In the 1930s, too, watchmakers were perfecting water-resistant watches to different depths and by the mid-1930s, chronograph wristwatches enabled long-term time recordings (hours and minutes). By the end of the 1930s, the dual push-button chronograph came into fashion. One button started and stopped the chronograph hands and the other returned them to zero. The 1940s saw the introduction of larger sport watches with more detailed dials and bezels, showing as much information as possible. Between the 1940s and 1950s, square, rectangular and cushioned-shaped sport watches made their appearance on the scene, as did the first chronograph wristwatches to house telemeters, tachymeters and calendars.

In the 1960s oversized dials sporting different colored subdials emerged. Cases had accents such as coin edging and pushers on chronographs now came in square, not just round, designs. The 1970s saw an era of combination sport watches, in

TOP Hublot's Chronograph wristwatch with black rubber strap is a perfect sport timepiece. It is water-resistant to 50 meters, and houses a self winding mechanical movement.

ABOVE Piaget's Polo Key Largo chronograph is water-resistant to 200 meters, features an automatic movement and is housed in an 18K white gold case and bracelet.

LEFT From Parmigiani Fleurier, this automatic chronograph wristwatch features a movement with tenth-of-a-second timer and calendar. It is available in 18K rose, or yellow gold, or in platinum.

RIGHT From Daniel Jean Richard, this TV-time chronograph is inspired by a 1940s design. It features a cushioned square case in steel, with copper dial and softly elegant blued hands for subtle sports appeal.

FAR RIGHT From Bell & Ross, the Space One chronograph timepiece was worn in space by Russian cosmonauts.

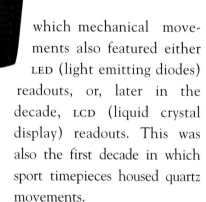

which mechanical movements also featured either LED (light emitting diodes) readouts, or, later in the decade, LCD (liquid crystal display) readouts. This was also the first decade in which sport timepieces housed quartz movements.

By the 1970s, and into the 1980s and 1990s, chronograph wristwatches had taken the world by storm. No longer were these timepieces instruments for professionals only; rather they became known as wonderfully rugged, fun sport watches that told a lifestyle story on the wrist. In the

1970s watchmakers introduced colored strap chronograph wristwatches in bold reds, blues and greens. By the 1980s this color scheme had progressed into a rainbow of hues and moved to cover not just the strap but the dials and subdials alike. With the chronograph "craze" in full swing, and with no end in sight, watchmakers in the 1990s needed only to be creative in design and style.

Over this century, too, as athletes and adventurers alike embarked on their quests, they made their own personal choices about which watch to wear on their wrists. It was in 1926 that Rolex made world headlines on the wrist of Mercedes Gleitze, who swam the English Channel that year wearing the Rolex Oyster, the first waterproof watch.

In 1927, Charles A. Lindbergh created the Hour Angle watch, which he designed after setting two records in the first nonstop New York-to-Paris flight in Spirit of St. Louis.

In 1930, Longines supplied a chronometer wristwatch to Hans von Schiller, the pilot of the first dirigible balloon, on his journey around the world. In 1937, Amelia Earhart strapped an Omega watch to her wrist when she set off to circle the globe. In 1945, General Eisenhower purchased a Heuer chronograph wristwatch to be sure his timing was exact. In 1947, Chuck Yeager wore a Rolex Oyster on his wrist as he flew faster than the speed of sound. It was a Rolex watch that was strapped on Sir Edmund Hillary's wrist in 1953 when he led the first successful expedition to the top of Mt. Everest.

A decade later, a Breitling was on the wrist of Lt. Commander Scott Carpenter in 1962 during the Mercury program. The Omega Speedmaster was on the wrist of Neil Armstrong when he stepped on to the moon's dusty Sea of Tranquility on July 21, 1969, and it was an Omega Speedmaster that enabled the module pilots of Apollo XIII to properly time the firing of their rockets for reentry into the earth's atmosphere in 1970 after an on-board explosion. It was a Bell & Ross wristwatch that was on the wrist of Reinhart Furrer in the Spacelab mission in 1983. A little more than a decade later, in 1994, Fortis watches held up to the rigors of spacewalks on the wrists of two cosmonauts during the Soyuz TM 19 mission.

Today, sports enthusiasts and modern-day adventurers utilize chronographs to time their practices or

ABOVE LEFT For those who cross barriers often, Franck Muller's Capital Time sport chronograph offers the time in 14 cities around the world.

LEFT Perrelet's limited series of 100 Louis-Frederic Perrelet split-seconds chronographs features hand-engraved automatic movements. These timepieces were made in tribute to the brand's founder, an early contributor to watchmaking technology credited as the inventor of the split-seconds mechanism in 1827.

BACKGROUND Emelia Earhart

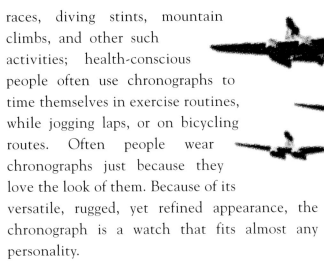

races, diving stints, mountain climbs, and other such activities; health-conscious people often use chronographs to time themselves in exercise routines, while jogging laps, or on bicycling routes. Often people wear chronographs just because they love the look of them. Because of its versatile, rugged, yet refined appearance, the chronograph is a watch that fits almost any personality.

Today's chronographs are sleek in design, and are available with either mechanical or quartz movements. Some chronographs even utilize combination movements, putting together quartz and either mechanical or electronic movements in one timepiece. Some chronographs offer digital readouts in addition to analog timekeeping functions. Many chronographs today also tout chronometer certifications (signifying that they have been tested under a series of very rigorous and stringent standards in the areas of pressure, durability, etc., and are certified to have passed). It is not unusual to find a chronograph with a pulsimeter to measure pulse rate, a tachymeter to measure speed or a telemeter to measure distance. Some companies even build in compasses and slide-rule calculation functions.

Of course, not every sport wristwatch must be a chronograph. For the mountain climber, swimmer, aerobics hound, or sports enthusiast not engaged in direct competition, split-second

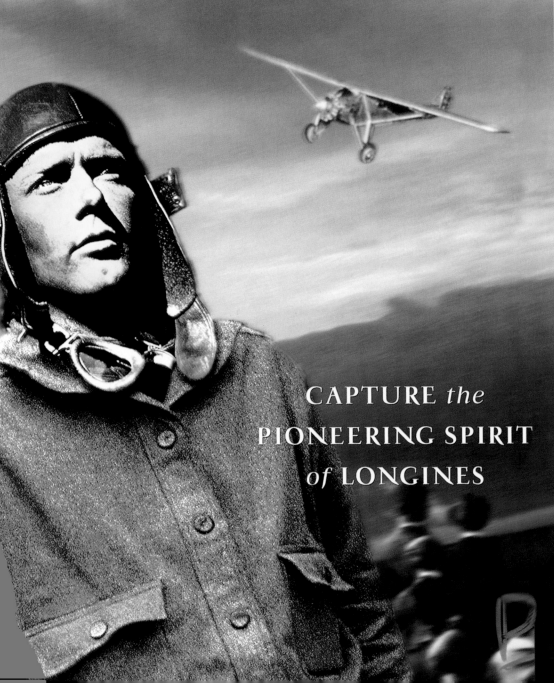

CAPTURE *the* PIONEERING SPIRIT *of* LONGINES

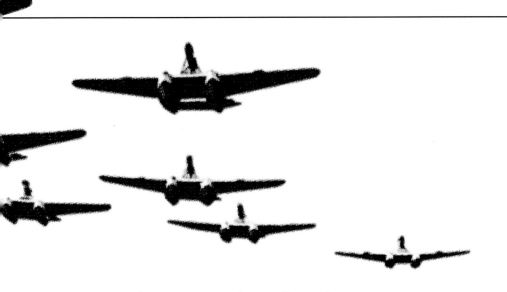

timing is a less important factor. Instead, some sports enthusiasts look for other characteristics to define a timepiece as a sport watch. Factors such as chronometer certification, durability, water resistance, anti-magnetism, and case and bracelet materials are key. Additionally, a sport watch can have functions that are germane to the indi- vidual's needs, such as an alarm, moon phase indicator, calendar, perpetual calendar, power reserve indicator (a function in mechanical wristwatches that tells how much power is left before the watch needs to be wound), or dual time zone functions.

Watchmakers continually endeavor to offer the most reliable product. For sport watches to-day, surgical grade stainless steel and titanium are most often the metals of choice for cases and bracelets, but some watchmakers also use high-tech composites such as engineering ceramic for sport watches. If straps are used, they are most frequently either rubber, neoprene or other composite, shark skin, or durable leather. Watchmakers are careful to take into considera-

tion special needs for specific sports, and so for the skier, diver, or other adveturer who likes to wear his or her watch over bulky attire, they have developed interchangeable bracelets, straps and extensions.

With regard to the water-resistance factor, watchmakers are careful to equip their specific timepieces with a variety of features, many of which are patented. Such features include double- or triple-locked winding crowns, additional gaskets for water resistance, helium escape valves, silicone "o" rings, glare-proof crystals, extra large crowns, luminescent hands and markers, graduated one-way rotating bezels that click into place, and double locked bracelet clasps. Watchmakers offer timepieces that are water-resistant to depths anywhere from several

FACING PAGE, TOP The Avigation collection of sport watches by Longines consists of automatic chronographs, power reserve indicator and calendar. In keeping with the latest sport timepieces, the watches feature mineral crystals, luminous numerals and hands and are water-resistant to 30 meters.

ABOVE The Eterna Pulsimeter Chronograph features not only chronograph and timekeeping functions, but also the ability to time the wearer's pulse to 30 pulsations. This new model is a replica of a pulsimeter chronograph created in 1942. It features domed sapphire crystal, a steel case and automatic movement with date.

LEFT The GST Aquatimer from IWC is a diver's watch that is pressure-proof to 2,000 meters. It is crafted in solid titanium or stainless steel and features a unidirectional rotating bezel and an additional Velcro strap for wearing the watch over the dive suit.

meters to thousands of meters, with crystals ranging from mineral to sapphire — all in an effort to please each individual sports enthusiast.

Ever since the First World War, watchmakers have been perfecting timepieces to traverse the skies without interruption. Early pilots were plagued by problems with magnetism, and watchmakers set to work finding methods to protect their movements from this force. A magnetic field, often encountered when flying, can throw the average mechanical watch completely off balance, confusing the escape wheels, balance rings, spring and other parts of the movement. Several master watchmakers in the field of pilot wristwatches addressed this problem by utilizing a soft inner iron

ring to house the movement, or by using a special alloy to conduct the magnetic fields — making anti-magnetic timepieces easily available.

Another key factor in sport watches is versatility and selection. For the avid skier, for instance, whose primary concern is weathering the slopes, water-resistancy and ruggedness are key. Durable steel or titanium watches are typically the first choice because watches are often banged against ski lifts and naturally get wet in spills. Some skiers prefer strap watches, shark skin or leather, because they don't get cold on the wrist, while bracelet believers feel that the metals weather the elements of cold and water better over time. Of course, for the professional skier, fraction-of-a-second timing is of the essence, as evidenced by a Rolex watch company ad that features Olympic skier Picabo Street succinctly summing things up: "In downhill racing, it's just you, the hill, and the clock."

*I*ndeed, not just with each different sport, but also with each goal or direction within a sport comes a different set of needs in timepieces. As a result, watch experts strive to offer both diversity and comprehensiveness in sport wristwatches. Some watch companies traverse the oceans, land and skies, while others specialize in particular arenas. Rolex, for instance, covers the realms of golf, automobile racing, diving and skiing. Similarly, Omega watches travel the depths of both the ocean and outer space, reaching even the moon — with stops on earth along the way. TAG-Heuer, a specialist on land, concentrates on skiing, automobile racing, and a variety of competitive sports. Breitling, although offering a variety of sport timepieces, is also known for its expertise in the field of aviation. Intimately involved in the world of automobile racing are Rolex, Girard-Perregaux, Franck Muller, Chopard and a host of other fine watch companies. The list goes on and on.

Some watch companies are not content to simply create sport watches, but also become more deeply involved in the sporting arena via sponsorships or timekeeping roles. Throughout the decades, many of the finest watch companies have held the role of Official Timekeeper of the

Olympic Games, as it is in the realm of the technically oriented sports — such as automobile racing, diving, yacht racing, and the Olympic Games — that many watchmakers prefer to focus. Often unable to resist the allure of matching technically precise items such as cars, planes, boats and rocket ships, watchmakers delve deeply into providing timepieces for these playing arenas.

With more than eighteen million recreational boats registered with the U.S. Coast Guard alone, the rapid growth of yacht racing and sailing presents a major opportunity for watchmakers. For those professionally inspired to race, or to sail distances that require nighttime navigation, tide information and the like, timepiece selec-

tions are limited. For the avid yachtsman, Corum Watch Company produces the well-known yachting watch called the Admiral's Cup. First introduced in the early 1960s, the Admiral's Cup is named for a yachting event that was started in 1957 by members of the Royal Ocean Racing Club of London. Today, there are a variety of Admiral's Cup timepieces, including the Admiral's Cup Regatta which is specially designed to calculate the start of a yacht race with precision. It includes a countdown device with five colored

disks that change in succession to help yachts-men maneuver during the ten minutes preceding the start of a race after the first gun.

For navigation, some companies create tide watches. Krieger's Tidal Chronometer, for instance, is preset to show the state of the tides and indicates the position of the tides at the wearer's particular port. The wearer can count the hours until the next high or low tide by way of graduations on the tide display. Ulysse Nardin's Astrolabium Galileo Galilei is an astronomical navigational tool that indicates the position of the sun, moon and stars. This wristwatch-sized astrolabe provides the wearer with exact information on the positions of the sun and the moon at any time of the day or night. There also are a wealth of nautically inspired sport watches on the market that do not offer celestial direction, tidal changes or regatta timing, but that are designed for the nautical lover. One such company is Hublot (French for "porthole"), whose signature case design stems directly from the porthole of a ship. The watch is offered with a rugged natural rubber strap that is impervious to water, and today there are chronograph and diver's versions. Audemars Piguet's Royal Oak is similarly characterized by its octagonal porthole bezel design with metal rivets; Patek Philippe's Nautilus timepiece is a porthole design with a more elliptical shape.

Wristwatches for in-water as well as on-water sports also command their own set of rules. While many divers agree that there is nothing as calm and peaceful as being 100 feet under the ocean, a degree of caution and concern is ever present. Divers are an interesting breed of people, taking their lives in their hands with every dive and relying on nothing but their own skills, knowl-

FACING PAGE, LEFT The Speedmaster Professional X-33 in titanium is fondly dubbed by Omega as the "Mars Watch." Designed and tested for five years in coordination with astronauts and professional pilots, it offers digital functions, including display of Mission Time. Timing to 1/100th of a second, the Chronograph is also a GMT watch and features an alarm mode and date in both international or English mode.

FACING PAGE, RIGHT The Saint Moritz chronograph from Chopard houses an automatic chronograph movement with 30-minute counters and independent small seconds hand. It has a date indicator, 43-hour power reserve and is water-resistant to 100 meters.

LEFT Gerald Genta's distinctive Night & Day watch offers a dual time zone function with night-and-day indicator.

edge and instruments. Wrist-watches are often part of that instrument category. For divers, timing underwater is critical. As such, consistency, durabil-ity, precision and water resis-tancy to the proper depths are absolute musts in a diver's wrist-watch. Often these wristwatches are the backup to a dive computer, acting as a quick-reference tool.

In the case of free-lake-diver Roland Specker, his watch was very important in helping him set a new world record. Specker, world-record holder in the "no-limits" category of lake diving (diving to 80 meters — approximately 240 feet — without oxygen support, using a cable and a cast-iron weight and resurfac-ing with an ascending parachute) recently set a new world record in the "variable weights" category — resurfacing assisted only by flippers. On his wrist, Specker wore the Omega Seamaster 300 Meter Chrono Diver watch to time his one-minute-and-forty-five-second round trip to sixty meters.

Another important underwater adventurer

BELOW In 1964 Heuer created the Carrera wristwatches in tribute to the Panamerican road races.

RIGHT This Daniel Roth chronograph is elegantly crafted in 18K gold for sleek appeal.

is Dr. Robert Ballard, who found the Lusitania and the Titanic, and who piloted the bathyscaphe Trieste in 1960 to the deepest point of the earth yet visited, the Mariana Trench. Strapped on the hull of the bathyscaphe, which reached a depth of 35,798 feet, was a specially made Rolex watch, which today continues to work and is on display in the company's New York headquarters.

In the opposite direction, the sky's the limit in pilot watches. While a good chronometer will suffice these days, watchmakers make sure to offer additional features in pilot wristwatches such as slide rule bezels, compasses, telemeter scales, tachymeters, GMT or dial time-zones, and anti-magnetic housing.

Among the specialists in air and

space are Omega, Fortis, Bell & Ross and Breitling. In 1942, in an effort to offer pilots the ability to make fast calculations, Breitling developed a chronograph with auxiliary dials and a calculator bezel that was called the Chronomat. Ten years later, in 1952, Breitling introduced the Navitimer, which offered chronograph functions, second-time-zone display and slide-rule bezel. Today, Breitling continues to create these pilot watches and more. Indeed, the list of aviator timepieces from Breitling reads like a what's what in pilot instruments. Breitling also takes a particular interest in supplying to aerobatic pilots around the world with specially created limited edition timepieces, making its list of wearers — the U.S. Air Force, Top Gun, U.S. Navy Fighter Weapons School, the Blue Angels of the U.S. Navy, Canada's Snowbirds, Britain's Royal Air Force, Japan's Blue Impulse — read like a who's who of aviation.

Wristwatches for land sports run the gamut as well, but one area that garners a great deal of attention from the watchmaking houses is the world of automobile racing and motor sports. Some watch companies recognized a certain synergy decades ago and struck up long-lasting relationships with the fast-paced, high-tech, romantic world of automobile racing. Others are only just entering the field as sponsors and time-keepers.

While much of the allure of motor sports is the exotic extremes and the high-tech machines capable of excessive speeds and rugged endurance, the finest watch companies in the world find this strangely akin to the technical prowess and perfection that is inherent in the finest mechanical wristwatches. Rolex affiliates itself with endurance racing, sponsoring The Rolex 24 at Daytona, one of the handful of major endurance races in the world. In tribute to the drivers who participate in the race, Rolex creates the Daytona timepiece in several versions. Another firm involved with endurance racing is Franck Muller, which has played host as the official watch and official timekeeper of the world's other great 24-hour endurance race: The Le Mans race, held annually in France. To celebrate its involvement, the firm

ABOVE From Oris, this ChronoOris Star timepiece, circa 1970, featured a tachymeter bezel.

LEFT The TAG-Heuer Monaco timepiece is a limited edition replica of the watch created decades ago and worn by Steve McQueen in the making of the 1970 movie *Le Mans*.

is its 1964 Heuer Carrera Chronograph. The reedition recalls the styling and design of the original 1964 Carrera, the origins of which date back to the 1950s when Jack Heuer cultivated a passionate interest in automobile racing. After competing in rallies, Heuer began competitive timekeeping in the United States for the 12 Hours of Sebring (analagous to the French Le Mans 24 Hours race) through which he became familiar with the Carrera Mexicana (also known as the Carrera Panamericana Mexico). Held five times from 1950 to 1954, this race covered 2,200 miles in nine stages stretching from the North American border to the Guatemalan frontier. Heuer created the Carrera in honor of this great challenge in automobile racing. Another car-affiliated timepiece from Heuer is the Monaco, a reedition of the 1969 Monaco chronograph with automatic winding that became hot when Steve McQueen wore it in the film *Le Mans* in 1970.

Chopard, while devoting considerably less time to the world of automobile racing, has nonetheless had a relationship with the Mille Miglia that has lasted more than a decade. Originally staged from 1927 to 1957, the Mille Miglia

created the Endurance 24 line of timepieces.

TAG-Heuer is another great player in the automobile racing arena, and one of the earliest, as well, having enjoyed more than three decades of involvement in this realm. TAG-Heuer is the Official Timekeeper for all Formula 1 automobile racing worldwide, as well as the Indianapolis 500. Among the myriad of timepieces in the racing world that TAG-Heuer creates, one of the newest

covered one thousand miles of land on some of the most scenic roads in the hills of Italy. After a twenty-year respite because of a tragic racing incident, the race was recommenced in 1977. In 1988, Karl-Friedrich Scheufele, vice-president of Chopard and avid vintage car collector, made Chopard the main sponsor of the event, a title it has maintained to the present. To commemorate the relationship, Chopard has created the Mille Miglia collection of timepieces, a comprehensive series of sport chronographs and chronometers that feature the 1000 Miglia name on the dial.

There are a host of other relative newcomers to the world of motor sports that are strong

LEFT Modern and inventive, Hamilton's Khaki Quartz Chronograph offers fresh appeal with an unusual rubber and steel bracelet.

Tribute to Ferrari, the line of timepieces grows in tandem with the Ferrari appeal and allure. Among the most coveted of these timepieces are the F50 automatic chronograph with perpetual calendar for owners of the Ferrari F50s and the TdF in honor of the Tour Auto race. Every Ferrari watch bears the Ferrari horse logo and has some semblance of Ferrari's classic design and color .

Omega also lays claim to the blacktops, with two-time Formula 1 World Champion Michael Schumacher as one of its top ambassadors. Since the turn of the century, Omega has been intimately involved in sports timing in many fields, including the Olympic Games. In 1997-98, Omega was named the Official Timekeeper of the PPG CART (Championship Auto Racing Teams) World Series. In honor of its role, Omega introduced the Speedmaster CART Racing watch, which is worn by Michael Andretti.

Philippe Charriol, too, is a lover of automobile racing. A race car driver and ice racer, Charriol has been a primary sponsor and participant of motor racing around the world since 1992. In honor of an alliance struck between Charriol and Lamborghini — culminating in the "Philippe Charriol SuperSport Trophy," Charriol created a series of SuperSports sport watches. The first such timepiece was an automatic chronograph called Venturi, the make of Philippe Charriol's first competition car. The list goes on and on, featuring such names as Eterna — which is

ABOVE The Longines Hour Angle watch is made with aviators in mind. It was conceived of and developed by Charles Lindbergh in 1927 after his solo transatlantic flight.

ABOVE RIGHT The Conquistador from Franck Muller is a tonneau-shaped chronograph inspired by the Cintrée Curvex collection.

contenders nevertheless. Not wanting to be just a sponsor or licensee of a Ferrari event, Dr. Luigi Macaluso, former professional race car driver and head of Girard-Perregaux, struck a co-branding deal with the chairman of Ferrari that resulted in the "for Ferrari" line of limited-edition stream-lined wristwatches. Beginning in 1994 with the

owned now by the Porsche family, and is launching a line of Porsche Design timepieces — and Revue Thommen, whose European racing involvements have spanned decades as well.

Of course, there are a multitude of other watch companies producing sport watches, just as the realm of sports continues to grow. Today there are new events such as surf boarding contests, skate boarding contests, roller blading events and an entire array of other competitions still in the formation stages. Wristwatches from the master watchmakers of the world will be sure to keep pace.

BELOW From Bedat & Co. ref. No. 8 is an unusual modern chronograph crafted in steel. It features a mechanical movement with automatic winding and padded leather strap.

BELOW LEFT The Sportwave Chrono from Ebel boasts a technical design executed in steel or titanium. This chronograph also features a tachymeter scale on the bezel.

STARS IN TIME

OMEGA

TAG HEUR

OMEGA

PIAGET

GERARD GENTA

OMEGA

VAN CLEEF & ARPELS

DUNHILL

OMEGA

MOVADO

CHOPARD

CHOPARD

ESQ

BOUCHERON

ETERNA·MATIC
Golden Heart

HAMILTON

ESQ

VERSACE

AUDEMARS PIGUET

A solid reputation and a commitment to excellence are the cornerstones of the Swiss watchmaking tradition. For Audemars Piguet, a watch manufactory that crafts by hand only 15,000 timepieces a year, those qualities are held dear. "Acquiring a good reputation is a long, hard task; keeping it is no easier, as it is quickly and easily lost," were the words of its founders penned in 1875. Those words live on today as the firm's creed, guiding it into the 21st century. Formed as a union between two seasoned watchmakers, Jules Audemars and Edward Piguet, and based in Le Brassus, Switzerland, the manufacatory has long pioneered high-performance watch movements, building a reputation for distinctive designs and using the most superior materials available. Audemars Piguet's watchmaking tradition started early

young men to turn to the art of watchmaking, fueling the valley's horological reputation to such a degree that manufacturers in Geneva came to rely upon Le Brassus' handiwork. It was against this backdrop that the Audemars and the Piguet families began to build a tradition of high-precision craftmanship that would become legendary.

The firm of Audemars, manufacturers of ebauches and complicated mechanisms, began perfecting the quality of their products and making complete movements. Louis Audemars started to entertain the notion of combining under one roof the entire series of operations required for the manufacture of precision watches. Following his lead, his son Jules Audemars was initiated in the sixteenth century in Switzerland when the Huguenot ancestors of Jules Audemars, seeking refuge from persecution in France, settled in Le Brassus. They generated a modest income by farming in the summertime. During the long winters, they stayed indoors and focused on honing various crafts.

The industrious inhabitants of the Le Brassus valley gained a reputation for their dexterity and innovative flair in working with wood, glass and other materials. It wasn't until the eighteenth century, however, that the valley became synonymous with watchmaking after a certain precocious young man named Samuel Olivier Meylan returned from studying the watchmaker's craft in Geneva and returned to establish his own manufactory. His pioneering venture inspired others to do the same, thus ushering in a new era in Le Brassus. The success of Meylan and those who followed him motivated more and more

early into the fine craft of watchmaking and completed his apprenticeship in 1873. He fine-tuned his skills working as a finisher, putting the final touches on escapements of chronographs, calendar watches and repeaters. After building his own workshop in his parent's farmhouse, he quickly became known throughout Switzerland for his superior work and his small enterprise was soon overwhelmed with orders it did not have the capacity to fulfill. Audemars was forced to hire more workers, one of whom was Edward Auguste Piguet, who hailed from one of the oldest watchmaking families in the valley. Like the Audemars, the Piguet family subsisted on farming in summer and watchmaking in winter, but they also had an industrial-scale workshop that in 1790 was the first of its kind in the region.

*A*fter completing his education, Edward Piguet took a job as a finisher with the firm of Le Brassus, where he developed a close friendship with Jules Audemars. The two young men found that they shared similar ambitions and spent much time discussing more sophisticated ways of making complicated wristwatches. Six years after their initial encounter, they decided to join forces and opened their own manufactory. The House of Audemars Piguet was born on the 17th of December 1875.

Jules Audemars assumed the title of technical director while Edward Piguet oversaw the business side of the operation as commercial and financial director. To this day, the two families divide their responsibilities along those very lines.

The year Audemars Piguet came into being it manufactured its first Grand Complication with minute repeater, perpetual calendar with moon phases, minute counter and a split-second chronograph. The company swiftly gained notice for the originality of its designs as well as its impressive technological achievements. In 1911, Audemars Piguet introduced one of the first complicated jeweled wristwatches, masterfully set with diamonds and featuring a small ten-line caliber with a minute repeater and a distinctive center second hand.

After the deaths of both original partners, which occurred within the span of a year, the company continued on its path of excellence: in 1925, the firm debuted the world's thinnest pocket

ABOVE CENTER Royal Oak Offshore Automatic day, date and month in steel. Also available in gold and on strap. Ref. 25807.

ABOVE RIGHT Offshore scratch in steel. Ref. 25770.

ABOVE Offshore titane Ref. 25721Ti.

watch, measuring a mere 1.32mm. In 1946, the company followed suit with the world's thinnest wristwatch, boasting a 1.64mm movement and, in 1967, the company set a record with the thinnest automatic movement, measuring no more than 2.45mm and

ABOVE Audemars Piguet manufactory.

TOP Tourbillon II in gold. Ref. JA25873.

TOP RIGHT Millinary dual zone.

BOTTOM RIGHT Automatic "Grand Complication" in Platinum and Rose gold. Ref. 25806PR/O/0002.

housed in a 21-karat gold rotor. In 1970, Audemars Piguet had another triumph with the now classic Royal Oak. A symbol of ruggedness, the design is inspired by the porthole-shaped windows of British naval ships, which had adopted the name Royal Oak for a series of its vessels. The name has been traced back to British King Charles II, who managed to escape from pursuers by seeking refuge in a giant oak.

*I*n 1995, Audemars Piguet issued a commemorative 25th anniversary edition. In fact, the Royal Oak has enjoyed numerous editions, including the Royal Oak Jubilee with its ultra-thin automatic movement, the striking Royal Oak Offshore and the Royal Oak Chronograph. New materials and complicated features have been added to this highly versatile model, including automatic perpetual calendar, dual time and phases of the moon.

But the Royal Oak is not the company's sole signature piece. The Triple Complication presented in 1992 enjoyed instant success, in

increasingly thinner and more delicate models include such classics as Carnegie, Opera, Grande Dame and Roberta — designed to "capture the feminine universe, its moods, its sensitivity and its flights of fancy." The great industrialist Andrew Carnegie also inspired the Audemars Piguet engineers who perfected the flat movement: the ML caliber developed in 1946 had a nine-line diameter and a thickness of 1.64mm.

Combining the best of the classic and the new, the Millinery line, recently introduced by the company is based on a horizontal oval. The case accommodates a complex movement with easy-to-read display and includes an inertia block balance for protection and reliability.

One of the first companies to expand its public exposure by sponsoring sports and fund-raising events, Audemars Piguet has fascinated collectors, the rich, the famous and discerning enthusiasts alike — a tradition that will continue along with the watchmaker's absolute commitment to excellence.

BELOW Millenary Acier Collection.

BOTTOM Millenary Gary Kasparov.

BOTTOM CENTER You and Me.

keeping with the manufactory's tradition of excellence. The Triple Complication is the crowning achievement of modern watchmaking. One of the most complicated instruments in the industry, only five of the remarkable timepieces are crafted each year. Its 600 hand-assembled parts activate a perpetual calendar allowing for self-adjusting leap years, a minute repeater and a split-second chronograph. It is housed in an 8.55mm-thick case with an 18-karat gold rotor and is available in a variety of contemporary designs.

The John Shaeffer minute repeaters are no less striking for their originality. Created in 1907 for a wealthy American industrialist who was fascinated with the musical complication, the initial model bore letters that spelled his name a character at a time on each index. The watch strikes on the hour, the quarters or each minute and hammers the time in two tones.

Audemars Piguet also used its early watchmaking and marketing genius to advance the cause of ladies' timepieces. The company's

BEDAT & C⁰

he newest upstart in the watch industry is a puzzle in time: How does a maiden watch brand exude the intelligence, elegance and prestige of a brand that has existed for hundreds of years? It helps, certainly, if its founders are long-time industry denizens, as is the case with Simone and Christian Bedat, the mother and son team who in 1997 launched Geneva's newest watchmaker. Simone Bedat is renowned as the co-founder of Raymond Weil, the same watchmaker that also groomed Christian Bedat, and BEDAT & CO is the culmination of decades of experience, even at the tender age of two years old. The premier collection of fifty-two watches caused quite a sensation at the watch and jewelry show in Basel. Not just because the Bedats are seasoned professionals in the watchmaking industry, but also because

of the incredible time frame in which the duo developed three distinctive lines. "It was quite a big challenge to create a concept, not just a watch but something that makes sense, in six months," recalls Christian Bedat.

Launching any business in less than a year is a daunting prospect, and in the highly specialized and serious world of Swiss watchmaking, virtually unimaginable. In order to create a successful line of watches the Bedats had to first discover their niche. After assessing the market, they perceived a gap in the luxury line that they knew they had the experience to fill. "We've created a very strong, understated product that is elegant and timeless. The watches are nice today, but they could have easily existed 10 or 15 years ago," says Christian Bedat, who conceptualizes each line.

Inspired by the work of artisans during the 1930s, the collection begins with the decidedly feminine line, number 3. Its faces curve sensuously in barrel, hexagonal or round shapes that hug the distinctive BEDAT & CO watch face. Perhaps most unique among the striking collection is the bracelet watch. "It's more a bracelet than a watch. It looks like a bracelet, like your grandmother's bracelet," says Christian Bedat. He continues to imprint an individualistic

stamp throughout the collection. The exploration of steel and gold is unmistakably elegant and individual. In one instance, a charcoal watchface is surrounded by gold bezel and linked together with a steel bracelet.

*F*or the man who is searching for an understated but captivating classic timepiece with a modern touch, the collection number 7 offers numerous choices to fit all personalities. The expansive collection grew even larger in 1998, with an exceptional chronograph version, in which each measure is housed in a small, rectangular-shaped window. Those seeking sportier versions can opt for collection number 8, whose round faces contain classic faces or chronographs.

It seems natural to name each line in the same manner in which time is expressed, in numbers. The inspiration spans the realm of symbolism. Christian Bedat, who spent several years working in Hong Kong, is also expressing a Zen for Eastern thought. In Asian philosophy, the number 8 represents prosperity, and it is one aspect of the enigmatic emblem for BEDAT & CO, the superimposed B which also resembles a figure eight, or an hourglass. The number 8 is endowed with great significance: on every watchface, 8 o'clock is replaced with the watchmaker's logo.

Just as a rose is a rose, each BEDAT & CO timepiece is distinctive for its familial and fresh characteristics, whether it is a round chronograph, or a lady's elegant dia-

ABOVE (LEFT TO RIGHT) No. 3 series of timepieces; in all steel, center in steel with 18K gold case, and above right in 18K gold.

FAR LEFT Automatic No. 7 featuring 185 diamonds, in steel with a black satin bracelet.

BELOW BEDAT & CO boutique in Dubai. One of a line of exclusive presentation boxes, created for BEDAT & CO by Links of London.

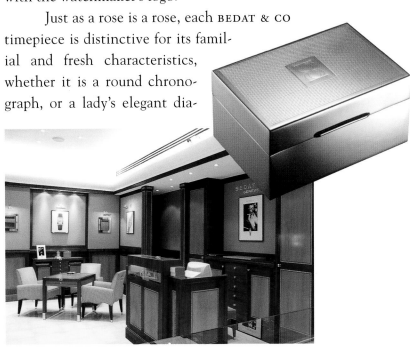

cept, otherwise you can find yourself going in any direction. There are few very good designers, and they have their own distinctive taste that you can often detect in different brands. That's what I don't want to happen with our collection," says Christian Bedat. "The only way to maintain our brand image in the long term is to insure that the input from the style comes from us. It's very important."

*U*ltimately, there is no mistaking a BEDAT watch. "When you look at our watch, you don't see the details, it is very discreet," explains Christian Bedat. Such fastidious attention indulged upon the time-pieces creates details that seem to have evolved over centuries. "The company name is always found on the top of the watchface, not under the 12 but above the 12. Our logo is always found at 8 o'clock, the watch hands are always BEDAT hands, in timepieces featuring a window

mond pavé bracelet, or a gallant men's rectangle watch. The mark of BEDAT & CO is discreetly incorporated in the design. Peer closely to see the name BEDAT & CO on the interior dial. Pore over the crown, the fine leather watchband, the clasp and witness how the watchmaker's identity is woven into every aspect of the timepiece, sublimated as part of the design.

"You have to know what to do and where you want to go when you create the design con-

for the date, the 8 is replaced by our logo, and then in the center of the dial you can read BEDAT & CO AOSC," Christian Bedat breathlessly explains before adding that AOSC is a set of guidelines developed by BEDAT & CO itself that guarantees that every component of every BEDAT & CO timepiece is made in Switzerland. Anything less wouldn't meet the level of standards that the Bedats have established for themselves, and it allows the watchmaker to guarantee its timepieces for five years, a longer stretch than BEDAT & CO has been in existence!

ABOVE BEDAT & CO manufactures in the Swiss Jura mountains.

ABOVE LEFT Automatic No. 7 in steel with blue or black dial.

LEFT Automatic No. 8 Chronograph, screwed crown and caseback in steel with leather strap.

BOUCHERON

Long before the wristwatch became common, Parisian jeweler Frederic Boucheron was already creating ornately designed timepieces, some worn as pendants or necklaces, others as true watches for the wrist. In 1858, at the height of the Second Empire — France's great age of luxury — Boucheron opened his first atelier and began creating timepieces adorned with gold, diamonds, sapphires, rubies and ceramics. During this era, watches were prized more for their beauty than their practicality. For women of the elite, whether aristocracy or social luminary, a Boucheron watch was often the final touch of one of the jeweler's famous "wedding sets" of rings, necklaces, earrings and bracelets. The timepiece was an exciting area of exploration for Boucheron, and the master jeweler's early creations

still have the power to surprise and delight; in his own time, observers remarked on Boucheron's ability to avoid the banal. In 1893, he opened his now-famous boutique in the Place Vendome, giving timepieces equal billing with his magnificent jewelry in the main show window. His designs of this period — involving scrolls, leaves and flowers, sinuous and chased in gold — helped define the emerging art nouveau movement Boucheron's master metalworkers and designers also began to create platinum timepieces far lighter and easier to wear than the offerings of other jewelers.

Following Frederic Boucheron's death, his son Louis took over the family business, and led the firm into the next important period of design: art deco. Natural motifs were supplanted by more geometric designs and a bold use of color. Louis Boucheron made a major contribution to art deco by perfecting the latest methods of stone-cutting and popularizing the use of lapis lazuli, onyx and turquoise.

Watches were a particularly good canvas upon which to experiment with the art deco style because of the geometric design of the face.

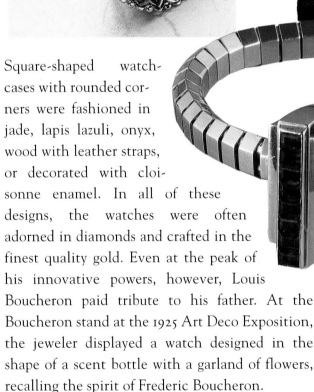

Square-shaped watchcases with rounded corners were fashioned in jade, lapis lazuli, onyx, wood with leather straps, or decorated with cloisonne enamel. In all of these designs, the watches were often adorned in diamonds and crafted in the finest quality gold. Even at the peak of his innovative powers, however, Louis Boucheron paid tribute to his father. At the Boucheron stand at the 1925 Art Deco Exposition, the jeweler displayed a watch designed in the shape of a scent bottle with a garland of flowers, recalling the spirit of Frederic Boucheron.

Some two decades later, after the end of World War II, Boucheron released a watch featuring one of the company's most important innovations — the patented invisible clasp. The strap is detachable from each side of the watchface and the and the watchband appears seamless, with no apparent beginning or end. This unique system allows the strap to be changed easily to match dif-

OPENING PAGE Boucheron's Boutique on the Place Vendôme.

PREVIOUS PAGE Rectangle-shape haute jewelry watch in 18K gray gold set with diamonds.

FACING PAGE Early examples of timepieces created at Boucheron.

TOP LEFT Ladies' watch, pierced gold with colored gemstones on a rope chain bracelet. 1953.

TOP RIGHT Wristwatch with diamonds and onyx on platinum. Silk moire strap. 1924.

ABOVE Fan watch set with diamonds and sapphires on gold, 1942.

LEFT Gents' chronograph in gold on a leather strap. 1945.

ABOVE Rectangle gadroon watches with
cultured pearl bracelets.

RIGHT 140 year's anniversary of
Boucheron watches set in grey gold with
a black crocodile strap.

BELOW Square shaped watches in 18K
yellow gold and gray gold.

FACING PAGE, TOP LEFT Yellow gold watch,
pavé dial on a yellow gold bracelet.,

TOP RIGHT Yellow gold watch and bracelet
set with diamonds, white mother-of-pearl
dial. Diamond set white gold watch.

LEFT *Magdalena* watch. Diamonds set in
gold with an interchangeable bracelet of
sapphires and diamonds on gold.

BOTTOM RIGHT *Magdalena* watch.
Diamonds set in gold with red crocodile
strap set with diamonds and gold. *Emma*
watch. Diamonds set in gold with honey-
colored crocodile bracelet set with diamonds and gold.

ferent outfits, and during the post-war era, stylish women seized on the innovation. Fashion dictated that a woman should change accessories to match each of her daily outfits: morning, afternoon and evening.

Complementing women's beauty is the essential mission of Boucheron's collections, according to Alain Boucheron, great-grandson of Frederic and current Chairman of Boucheron. The company's two basic watch lines — one with round, the other with rectangular-shaped faces — both bear the "gadroon," a series of curved grooves "which follows the flowing curves of a woman's body," explains Boucheron. "Everyone can appreciate the beauty of a woman, and this inspiration is shown in the harmony of the curves. These curves are seen throughout our collection of jewelry, watches and the bottles housing our perfume."

*B*oucheron also features a collection of square watches based on a timepiece created in 1952. With a wealth of fabled timepieces in its archives, Boucheron naturally receives many requests to reissue such time-honored models. While some of these requests are honored, Alain Boucheron says the company must maintain a balance between its history and its future.

"When a company has a great past, they must be careful not to place too much reliance on earlier designs and spirit. Boucheron is perfectly adept at living with its renowned

past, yet moving forward," says Alain Boucheron. "We see the need for more discreet, simple designs. There is no longer the demand for 'flashy' jewelry. In haute jewelry, the designs remain consistently classical."

To celebrate its 140th anniversary, Boucheron created a special limited edition of 140 watches. The company joined efforts with Piguet, also celebrating its 140th anniversary. The commemorative watch is round, made of white gold with a sapphire-glass caseback displaying the mechanics of its automatic movement.

For the future, Alain Boucheron says that a third line of watches will be released, and the company is now focusing on developing distribution for all of its products. In 1996, Boucheron confirmed its watchmaking ambitions by displaying its timepieces at the Basel Trade Fair. Within the next three years, Boucheron

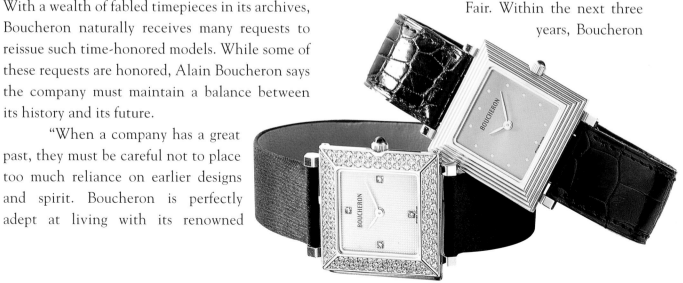

hopes
to greatly build on the company's international distribution, particularly in the United States. Most importantly, Alain Boucheron is committed to educating the world about the Boucheron family and tradition.

"Today, consumers want to know more about the company offering a product, and they want to identify with the company and its long-standing history," explains Boucheron. "People are becoming more discriminating and are seeking greater personal knowledge of the brand." Under his careful direction, the company's collections of timepieces will continue to display the same elegance and high style that began under his great-grandfather, and Boucheron watches will still be coveted by royalty, movie stars and connoisseurs who demand the finest quality.

BREITLING

For a watchmaker whose name defines a standard the world over and whose reputation spans more than a century, upholding the motto "making instruments for professionals" is a raison d'être. Producing some of the finest pieces of watchmanship, admired by professionals and lay people alike, Breitling has been perfecting the measurement of time with an unfailing expertise and mastery of precision that has also made its collaboration with the world of aviation legendary. It is the internationally favored timepiece of such aerobatic aces as the Blue Angels, the Thunderbirds, the British Red Arrows, the Patrouille de France, the Frecce Tricolori and has recently been named Official Chronograph of the American Airpower Heritage Group — the Confederate Air Force. The firm was founded 114

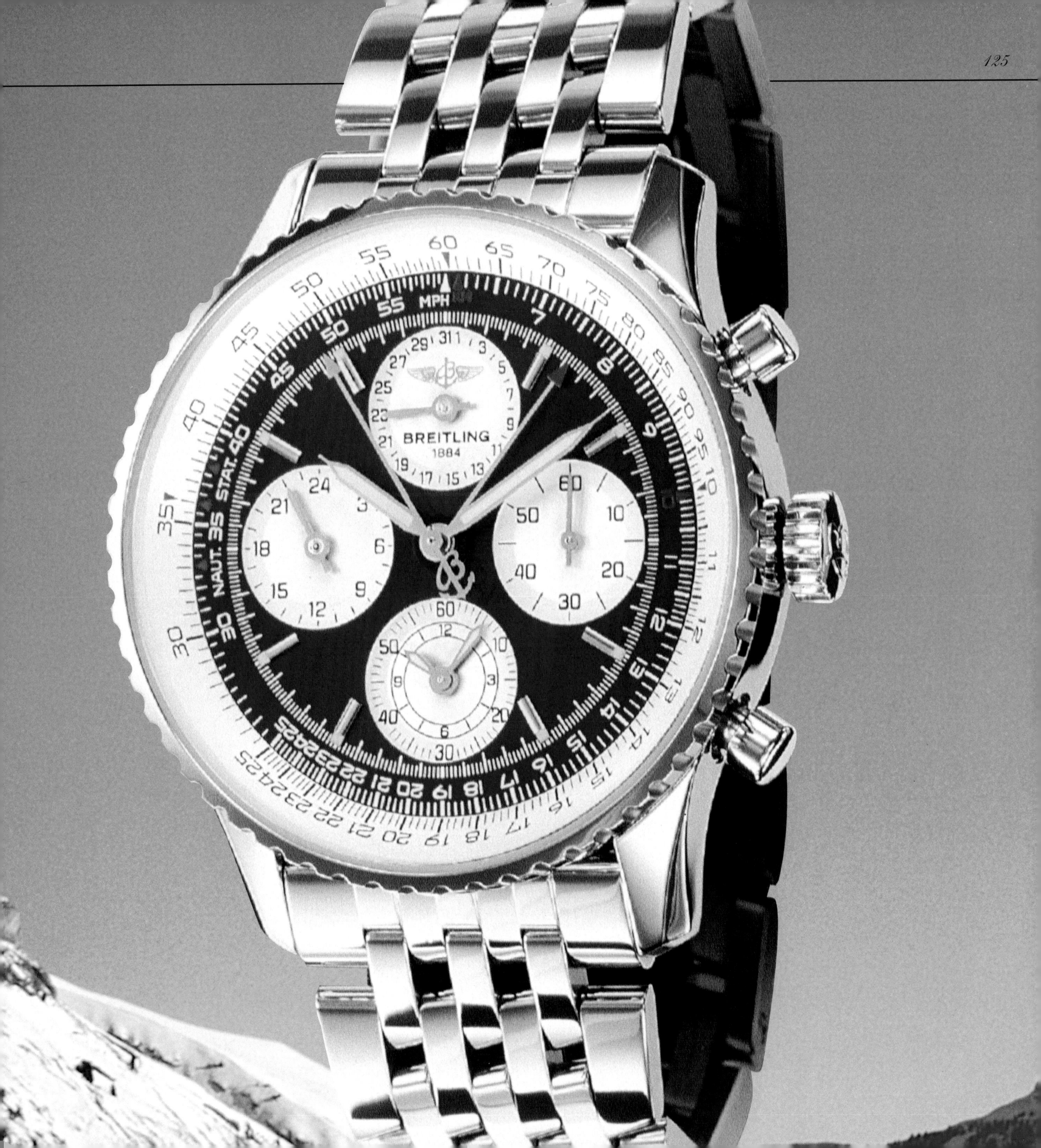
BREITLING
1884
MPH
NAUT.
STAT.

OPENING PAGE Breitling's Orbiter 2 crew set out in January of 1998 on Breitling's second attempt to set the last remaining aeronautical record by achieving the first nonstop round-the-world balloon flight.

PREVIOUS PAGE Twin Sixty.

ABOVE Following the Montbrillant QP and 1461 Days models, the Eclipse chrono-graph is the third part of the trilogy of Montbrillant complication models. The Montbrillant Eclipse displays the phases of the moon. The 18K rose gold or steel case is identical to that of the QP and 1461, in the classic Montbrillant style with its convex, glareproofed glass and the avia-tion slide rule which converts distances or units and handles all rule-of-three calculations.

RIGHT Chrono Jetstream.

years ago by Leon Breitling, who set out to build chronographs and stopwatches exclusively. The dexterous watchmaker was only twenty four when he opened his own workshop in the Swiss Jura and produced a chronograph bearing his name. In a period of substantial technical discovery, Leon knew that it was necessary to specialize in an industry that employed 40,000 people out of a population of 2.5 million; he proceeded to launch models with increasingly complicated hand-crafted movements. After only a few years in business, he swiftly gained recognition and won a series of prizes at expositions, firmly planting the Breitling name in the firmament of the Swiss watchmaking tradition.

By 1892, the firm had outgrown its facilities in Saint Imier and moved to La Chaux-de-Fonds, Switzerland's celebrated watchmaking center, where most of the firm's suppliers were located. Changing the firm's name to Leon G. Breitling s.a. Montbrillant Watch Manufactory, what had been a small workshop had now become a fairly large factory employing sixty people. When Leon Breitling died in 1914, the firm passed on to his son Gaston, who had been trained as a watch-maker and was well prepared to carry on what had become a prosperous business.

With the outbreak of the First World War, many markets closed and the ability to adapt to changing and uncertain times was critical. The forward-thinking Gaston decided to exploit the niche the firm had established for itself and went on to perfect the chronograph, the company's specialty product. The resulting Vitesse model met with extraordinary success and was later patented. The stopwatch, with its 30-minute indicator and center sweep hand, was immedi-ately snatched up by police departments which lost no time in using it to record theworld's first known speed offenders.

But Gaston's innovation did not stop there. He decided to take the stopwatch out of the waistcoat pocket and attach it to the wrist with a leather strap — a convenience that delighted both craftsmen and sportsmen, as well as military men who found the new watch an essential tool for measuring such vital things as how many revolutions a motor could make per minute or how far a vehicle could travel at a given speed. Breitling had also perfected a new breed of dials that could measure time-event situations. The ever newer dial layouts with special scales and calculations greatly expanded the firm's market and even went on to include the Unedeu, which was a pocket-watch counter with a three-digit display operated by a push button. The Church found this model especially useful — priests were known to use the watch to monitor the number of faithful who would show up at mass.

By the time Gaston died in 1927, the company had earned the distinction of being masters

ABOVE The "compact" Colt models— Chrono, Automatic and Quartz— have been completely redesigned and enhanced by significant technical innovations. Now nicknamed Ocean, the new Colt models are even more rugged and watertight to a depth of 500 meters (1,650 ft). Cases are in steel only, on leather, sharkskin, Diver, Diver Pro strap, or metal Fighter bracelet.

RIGHT In accordance with the requirements of aviation professionals, the B-One includes only essential functions: alarm, perpetual calendar, chronograph split and add functions, countdown timer, second timezone with its own alarm, UTC time and aviation slide rule. Optimal time readout is ensured by oversized hands and nighttime backlighting of displays which is NVG-compatible (night-vision goggles).

ABOVE Superocean Professional has a high degree of watertightness: it is able to withstand pressures of 150 atmospheres or a depth of 1,500 meters (5,000 ft.) The watch meets military requirements in the field and its matte finish will not attract potentially aggressive sea creatures. The case is fitted with a decompression valve to guard against explosion upon reaching the surface.

RIGHT Chronomat GT.

of a precision science. The firm was credited with having produced what were essentially the first "mini-computers": watches that could tell you everything from the time to the answer to a math equation. With the rise of aeronautics in the early twentieth century, no watchmaking firm was better poised to meet the technological demands of an equally exacting industry. In the 1930s, Breitling was named official supplier to the Royal Air Force and in 1942 launched the now legendary Chronomat, a two-register chronograph with a revolving bezel and a complete logarithmic slide-rule. It was not surprising that it quickly became indispensable to pilots who used it not only to see what time it was, but to calculate fuel consumption, air speed, and estimated arrival times.

With the dawn of commercial aviation in 1952, Breitling's association with aviation was unparalleled. As the first Lockheed 110-passenger Super Constellation lifted into the air, Breitling was also making headlines with its latest innovation, the Navitimer, a three-subdial chronograph with an improved slide rule on the outer bezel, "a bezel with talent" as the company likes to say. It was fitting that the AOPA, the Aircraft Owners and Pilot's Association, declared the Navitimer its official watch because it met the rigorous demands of air navigation so admirably.

But it wasn't until ten years later that the firm's crowning piece was to make history. On May 24, 1962, astronaut Scott Carpenter, sporting the Navitimer, was hurled 272 km into space from a rocket in Cape Canaveral, effectively subjecting himself and his watch to an eight fold increase in the force of gravity. Both performed exceptionally, especially when the capsule's re-entry into the atmosphere forced Carpenter to manually pilot his spacecraft back to earth. His eyes glued to his watch, Carpenter used the slide rule to calculate the exact position of his reentry. When he splashed down safe and sound 300 km away from his intended spot, he pulled off one of the space program's most heroic feats, making a legend of himself and his timepiece. Soon thereafter, Carpenter's Navitimer was aptly rechristened the Cosmonaute and still remains at the forefront of the company's line.

Thirty years later, the Cosmonaute sits on the wrist of many an airman, not to mention distinguished watch enthusiasts. Breitling has preserved the grand tradition and has recently developed a whole line of specialized chronographs which include the Navitimer Quantieme Perpetuel and the Navitimer Rattrapante.

The Cosmonaute II most resembles Carpenter's watch and is the only modern-day Breitling fitted with a hand-wound mechanical movement with the dial divided into 24 hours. The dial remains unchanged: large Arabic numerals with interspersed markings.

Then there is the Montbrillant Eclipse, a chronograph which is the third part of the trilogy of the Montbrillant complication models. With a

ABOVE LEFT The Colt Chrono Ocean's case construction is designed to offer maximum shock-resistance and to prevent premature deterioration. The high-performance electronic quartz movement measures to 1/10th of a second, indicating split and add times, and has a rapid time-setting system (time zone, summer time).

RIGHT The Chronoracer Rattrapante is an exceptional chronograph that utilizes electronics and mechanical engineering offering the reliability of a quartz-driven movement and the control of a mechanical chronograph.

ABOVE LEFT Montbrillant QP

ABOVE CENTER Montbrillant 1461

ABOVE RIGHT Montbrillant Eclipse

RIGHT In order to give broader scope to the Breitling Academy, a basic scholarship will be awarded to a hundred young people, all of whom share the common goal of a determination to fly.

simpler though no less original design, the Montbrillant displays the various stages of the moon as it revolves around the earth. The 25-jewel Breitling Caliber 43 houses a chronograph module with a 1/5th-of-a-second counter and 30-minute totalizer. The mechanism displaying the perpetual cycle of the moon is integrated in the spot normally reserved for the hour counter. The 18-karat gold or steel case is identical to that of the QP and 1461 in the classic Montbrillant style with convex glare proof glass and the aviation slide rule converting distance and/or units.

Breitling's new generation of watches serves the needs of a rapidly expanding clientele in search of a well-designed, multifunctional watch to suit active lifestyles. In a striking new development, the three compact Colt models (nicknamed the Ocean models) have been completely redesigned. They are even more rugged than before and are water-resistant to 500 meters. The main features on the case have been improved: screw-locked crown, recessed crystal, crown guard, one-piece unidirectional bezel, oversized hands. The new Colt Chrono Ocean has undergone the same aesthetic transformations: the case construction is designed to offer maximum shock resistance and to prevent premature deterioration. The high performance electronic quartz movement measures time to

1/10th of a second, indicating split and add times and has optimal legibility. The Colt Superocean Professional is crafted in the same style as its predecessor, but has a increased degree of water tightness to pressures of 150 atmospheres. Its case is a matte finish that will not attract aggressive sea creatures. It also fulfills a set of military requirements and boasts a decompression valve that vents helium. The 3.7mm-thick glass can withstand pressures of up to one ton and is glareproof on either side.

The B-One, which has taken two years to develop, is a streamlined multifunctional chronograph designed for easy operation. In accordance with the requirements of aviation professionals, the B-One boasts only essential functions: countdown timer, second time zone and its own alarm, UTC time, aviation slide rule, oversize hands and nighttime backlighting. Its case is particularly unusual: an overdrive pinion mechanism operates the slide rule disk on the dial from the outside by rotating the bezel to ensure water resistance. The caseback, which resembles turbine blades, serves as a resonating chamber to amplify acoustic signals transmitted when functions are activated.

The Chronoracer Rattrapante is a shining example of the fusion of mechanical and electronic engineering. It offers the reliability of a quartz-driven movement as well as entirely mechanical chronograph control. A fly-back hand mechanism driven by a column wheel has been added and is one of the most refined complications a chronograph can house. The transparent caseback offers full views of this highly sophisticated complication. Shaped push-pieces have been added but the polished steel case remains faithful to the Chronoliner series.

Designed with the Breitling adventurer in mind, the watchmaker has launched the Emergency watch: an aerial pulls out from the watch can broadcast a radio distress signal and indicate the wearers precise location.

Breitling's Orbiter Team will again attempt to fly nonstop around the world. The three-man crew set records last winter while attempting to ride the jetstream around the globe in two weeks. At times, the Orbiter reached speeds of 300 mph, and seemed poised for a successful flight, but when China failed to issue timely clearance through its airspace, the crew was forced to end the mission early. They will set out again, this year, and you can be sure the engineers will be wearing their Breitlings.

LEFT Newest version of the Chronomat, Breitling's best-selling watch.

BELOW Orbiter crew.

CHAUMET

The art of creating great luxury is enhanced by experience. There are few jewelry and watch designers today as accomplished in that art as Chaumet. The Chaumet tradition that has been built since the age of Napoleon is the foundation of every item the company makes. Every Chaumet design — from the most classic to the most contemporary — has the knowledge of two centuries behind it. While Chaumet has devoted increasing attention to watchmaking over the past century, the company has been creating fine timepieces since its first years under its founder, Marie-Etienne Nitot. An early example is a pair of wristwatches made for Princess Augusta of Bavaria in 1811. Already having created the jewelry for her wedding to Prince Eugene de Beauharnais in 1807 (as well as crowns and insignia

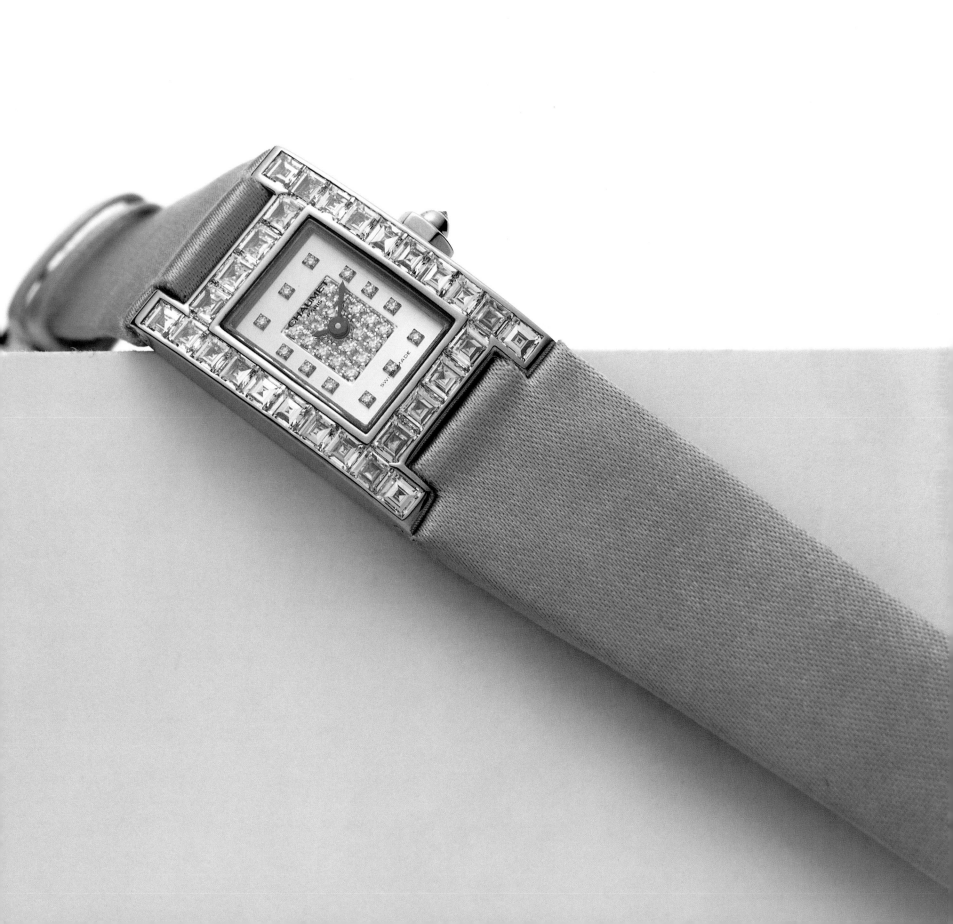

ated an extraordinary watch for Empress Marie-Louise. The watch hangs on a neck chain of twisted seed pearls and gold beads. The round gold case is enameled green, bordered with pearls centered on a crowned cipher "N" within a laurel crown. On the reverse, there is a bee framed in stars. The Empress presented the watch to Fanny Soufflot, companion of the King of Rome.

By the mid-1800s, the enterprise had passed on to the family of Jean-Baptiste Fossin, Nitot's foreman. In 1853, Jean-Baptiste's son, Jules Fossin, made a chatelaine and watch for the Empress to present as a gift to the Comtesse de la Bedoyere, also a customer of the Fossins. The chatelaine, designed as a looped blue ribbon edged with rose diamonds with a pearl in the center, holds a watch case enameled blue en suite bearing the Empress's crowned cipher executed in rose diamonds.

In the 1890s, Joseph Chaumet assumed control of the firm, giving the company the name by which it is known today. In 1910, from the shop's new location at 12

OPENING PAGE Chaumet store and salon, Place Vendôme.

PREVIOUS PAGE Style de Chaumet wristwatch in white gold set entirely with princess-cut diamonds, dial with pavé diamond center and diamond indexes on a pastel blue satin bracelet, quartz movement.

ABOVE Four Style de Chaumet - Pastels wristwatches, in steel with pavé diamonds and mother-of-pearl dials in pastel shades on matching satin bracelets, quartz movement.

TOP CENTER Style de Chaumet chronograph in yellow gold with pavé diamonds, green sapphire poussoirs and green mother-of-pearl dial on a green crocodile bracelet, quartz movement.

RIGHT Three Style de Chaumet wristwatches in yellow gold, large rectangular model on crocodile bracelet, small rectangular model with pavé diamonds on gold bracelet, small square model in plain gold with diamond indexes on the dial, quartz movement.

for her father, Maximilian I of Bavaria, and her mother, Queen Caroline), Nitot & Fils went on to make this set of matching watches — one for the time and one for the calendar. The bands are of delicate emerald and pearl scrolls, similar to bracelets of the time.

In 1813, Nitot's son, Francois-Regnault, cre-

Place Vendôme, Chaumet created a memorable collection of three lady's watches. The three flat round cases are enameled on engine-turned grounds in soft shades of green, blue and pink with rose diamond and colored stone details. They are fashioned to hang from a silk ribbon or from chains with links enameled to match, and are designed to nestle elegantly among the lace trimmings of a dress. One of Joseph Chaumet's finest creations is a 1924 Regency-style pendant watch made to hang on the lapel. The piece has a torpedo-shaped crystal top and a black enamel chain, with a round case in green and black contrasting with the glitter of tiny diamonds.

Today, the House of Chaumet designs watches to suit a broad scope of tastes and desires. The bejeweled masterpieces of Chaumet's past have been reenvisioned to complement a variety of contemporary lifestyles.

On the one hand, for instance, there is the timeless beauty of traditional styles such as the Khesis Classic Lady. This watch, with a yellow gold

TOP LEFT Style de Chaumet wristwatch in steel, large round model, quartz movement.

TOP CENTER Style de Chaumet chronograph in steel on a leather bracelet, black dial with numbers and indexes and tritium, quartz movement.

ABOVE Style de Chaumet wristwatch in steel, large square model with automatic movement and two-tone dial.

LEFT Two Style de Chaumet wristwatches in yellow gold, chronograph on a crocodile bracelet with quartz movement, large square model with two tone dial on crocodile bracelet with an automatic movement.

nograph, with its tastefully sporty approach. Its practicality and finesse have drawn widespread attention. It has an automatic movement, in steel with two-toned dial and tritium appliqué on a steel bracelet. There is also the dress version in white gold with pavé diamonds, mother-of-pearl dial and sapphire cabochon poussoirs.

The Chaumet watch collections are intimately linked with the company's

bracelet, has diamond-studded brancards, a white dial and diamond indexes. At the far end of the spectrum is the new Class One diving watch, in steel with a black dial and white numerals, on a rubber bracelet. The first diving watch for the French jeweler, the Class One is distinctly a weekend watch — sporty and water-resistant to 100 meters.

One timepiece whose popularity has been increasing is the Style de Chaumet chro-

extensive line of fine jewelry. The Anneau watch in gold surrounded by a brilliant bouquet of multicolored sapphires can be worn with a ring of the same design. Many of the watches of the Khesis line, particularly the ones surrounded in diamonds, resemble elegant pieces of jewelry with their small faces and bright gold or steel bands. There are rings and bracelets to match.

Chaumet also produces a range of watches with simple, clean designs. There are round, square and rectangular watches, with roman numerals, Arabic numerals or diamonds as indicators. There are straps made of gold, steel, calfskin, crocodile, black patent leather and diamonds; an array of satin straps appear in green, yellow, pink or blue.

TOP LEFT Inès Sastre wears a Khésis Top Lady wristwatch in white gold with pavé diamond center dial and a matching Khésis diamond ring in white gold with square motif set with princess-cut diamonds.

ABOVE Khésis Top Lady wristwatch in yellow gold with roman numerals on a white dial, Khésis Classic Lady also in yellow gold with pavé diamonds and diamond indexes, quartz movement.

BOTTOM LEFT Two Khésis wristwatches in steel, Classic Lady with pavé diamonds and white dial, Top Lady with black dial and diamond indexes, quartz movement.

Pierre Haquet, the present CEO of Chaumet, is determined to move forward with the development of new and exciting designs. He credits the high standards of quality that the company has maintained over its more than two centuries of existence for the success it continues to enjoy today.

CHOPARD

R ipe with explosive creative energy and technical know-how, Chopard is emerging as a major driving force in the world of watchmaking. Thriving on 138 years of experience in horology, the watchmaker and jeweler is perpetually reinforcing its status as a "manufacture," a word more precious than gold in the Swiss watchmaking community. What it means, to skilled craftsmen and proud watchmakers, is that the company itself creates its own caliber, hand-working and hand-crafting each part of the beating heart of a timepiece. It is a level that few in the industry attain and the path toward becoming a manufacture is not only arduous, but it requires the intricate, highly specialized knowledge of how to build a mechanism that will power a timepiece. For this reason, the year 1997

PREVIOUS PAGES Chopard Vice-President Karl-Friedrich Scheufele drives Carla Bruni in a 1955 A Spyder Porsche 550 during the Mille Miglia. Under Karl-Friedrich Scheufele's direction, Chopard has sponsored the race for ten years. The 1998 commemorative chronograph watch is racy with its rubber bracelet featuring the Dunlop racing tire design.

TOP, LEFT TO RIGHT Mille Miglia collection over the years: in 1988, 1991, 1993, and 1995.

ABOVE Sonvilier, the village where Chopard was founded in 1860.

BOTTOM, LEFT TO RIGHT Louis-Ulysse Chopard, 1860, in the center; Karl Scheufele in New York in 1925; Louis-Ulysse Chopard with his son and grandsons ; Chopard in Sonvilier, 1860; Chopard in Fleurier today.

became a landmark for Chopard, one of the last family-owned watchmakers in Switzerland. With the premier of LUC 1860, the company began harnessing hundreds of years of steady momentum that began when Louis Ulysse Chopard opened his watchmaking company in the mountains in 1860, and declared that he would be creating the best precision watches in Sonvilier, Switzerland. Known as an expert in the production of calibers during his time, Chopard's reputation earned him the position of main supplier to the legendary Swiss railways. Chopard prospered for the next two generations before the family's passion for watchmaking waned. The watchmaker's distinguished reputation led Karl and Karin Scheufele, descendants of longtime watchmakers and jewelers, to buy the company in 1963.

For the past decade, Karl-Friedrich Scheufele has assumed the mission established by Louis Ulysse Chopard: to produce Switzerland's finest watches. Karl-Friedrich oversees the development of men's watches at Chopard and also shares

the vice-presidency with his sister, Caroline Gruosi Scheufele, who designs the company's jewelry and jeweled watches. It was Karl-Friedrich's quest to develop a movement in tribute to Chopard's founder that fueled the project, and he proudly notes that the development of the LUC movement is a resounding success.

"There is a tremendous backlog and all of the 16/1860 movements are sold out for one to one-and-a-half years," says Karl-Friedrich Scheufele. His dedication sustained the lengthy and costly project through difficult and uncertain times. Chopard's chief engineers spent three years developing and producing the movement. Riding the wave of inspiration, Chopard is revising and updating LUC 1860; the newest feature is a center seconds hand. The Chopard family established the workshops in Fleurier in 1995, just 40 kilometers from Ulysse Chopard's original workshops, and within two years 20 craftsmen were employed and a movement premiered. Immediately, it earned recognition for its virtuosity, and the men's watch won "Watch of the Year" from a panel of specialized journalists and watch retail-

ers. Now, 2,000 calibers are crafted each year, with plans underway for the development of new movements.

This is only the beginning of the fresh dynamism that is electrifying the atmosphere at Chopard's headquarters in Meyrin, Switzerland, just outside of Geneva. Both Karl-Friedrich and his sister Caroline are propelling Chopard into the millennium. Under the sage guidance of their parents, Chopard's new generation is leading the direction of design and craftsmanship in the same spirit that their parents had decades earlier.

The minute Karl and Karin Scheufele purchased Chopard, plans were underway for expansion that eventually landed them in the Meyrin facto-

The evolution of each of Chopard's collections is testimony to the spirit of reinvigoration. Witness the streamlined, newly redesigned Sports Collection, one of Chopard's first waterproof timepieces at its premier in 1980. "The men's version became more masculine, the lines straighter, there are less curves in the design, the watch is bigger and more aggressive looking," explains Karl-Friedrich. Crafted in steel with icy blue, white or copper-colored dials, the 1998 model is bolder and sleeker, yet it continues to reflect the refined, resolutely contemporary sports watch designed decades earlier. Nearly twenty years ago, Karl-Friedrich Scheufele took a daring risk as he attempted to convince a businessman that the Sports Collection timepieces were water-resistant. In the middle of dinner, he dropped one into an ice bucket, and two anxious hours later fished out the watch, still running.

TOP Perpetual calendar chronograph in platinum. The calendar indicates the day, date, month and year in accordance with the leap year, the phases of the moon and the seasons. In a limited issue of 50 in platinum, yellow gold and rose gold. The movement of this "chef d'oeuvre" contains no less than 478 parts.

RIGHT Tonneau with retrograde perpetual calendar. Over a month, the date indicator hand passes over the graduated semi-circle at 12 o'clock before returning to its point of departure and starting its perpetual motion again. The dial displays the date, month, year and phases of the moon.

ries in 1974. With the larger facilities, as well as the production in Pforzheim, and now its new movement manufacture in Fleurier, the Scheufeles have full control over every stage of development. Gold bars are delivered to Chopard's workshops in Geneva and melted down before becoming a piece of jewelry or watch case. Jewels are produced in Germany. Watch parts are manufactured in Fleurier. There is not one stage that relies on outside sources, leaving Chopard in a position of liberation to advance at its own speed and in its own direction.

Today's Sports Collection is waterproof to 100 feet, and the collection has expanded to include a self-winding movement and a 43-hour power reserve, which may also contain a chronograph. The sporty Mille Miglia is updated as Chopard celebrates its tenth anniversary as sponsor. The steel case chronograph features a rubber strap in the Dunlop racing tire design. Once again, sponsoring the 1,600-km race is the passion of Karl-Friedrich, who drove alongside renowned driver Jacky Ickx in a 1955 Spyder Porsche 550. Partly a competitive race, but mostly a leisurely drive through scenic country roads through Northern Italy, the Mille Miglia is a lovely spectacle for the drivers as well as the spectators, who come to see 370 classic cars built between 1927 and 1957. The 1998 commemo-

could diamonds float freely? The world's hardest substance would immediately scratch and ruin the watch crystal. Chopard's craftsmen spent countless hours puzzling over the riddle before finally solving the problem. Finally, engineers found the solution. By applying a thin sheath of gold to the back of each diamond, the craftsmen kept the diamonds from scratching the watch crystal. The joyous sparkle of floating diamonds is sure to bring a smile to anyone who wears the timepiece. Today the collection ranges from the "Happy Sport" to the "Be Happy" and "Happy Star" lines.

The "Be Happy" collection, a black plastic watchcase filled with sparkling diamonds, spurred Caroline Gruosi-Scheufele

rative Mille Miglia timepiece is produced in a limited edition of 1,000 steel watches and 100 18K gold watches.

The Happy Diamonds collection — whether mysterious with black diamonds, sporty in vibrant colors, or elegant with diamonds encircling diamonds — grows more exciting with each metamorphosis. By now, most are familiar with the celebrated tale of Chopard's designer, Ronald Kurowski, who in 1976 won the prestigious Golden Rose of Baden-Baden for his timepiece, inspired by the beauty of a waterfall. At first, the concept seemed impossible to execute. How

to proclaim, "I've created the first plastic Happy Watch." For her, the possibilities within the Happy Watch collection are endless. Specially for the International Cannes Film Festival, Caroline Gruosi-Scheufele created the "Happy Star" collection of 999 pieces, all crafted in midnight blue steel surrounding a mysteriously deep blue watchface, providing the perfect backdrop for the shimmer of floating diamond stars. With Happy Diamonds, happy days are here again, in particular for women, who now have abundant timepieces from which to choose.

Naturally, the growth of Chopard is flourishing, with plans to open exclusive Chopard boutiques, adding to twenty-five boutiques worldwide from Geneva to Athens, Baden-Baden, London, Paris, Vienna, Florence, Marbella, Münich, New York, Dubai, Hong Kong, Jakarta, Kuala Lumpur, Osaka, Singapore, Taipei, Tokyo and most recently, Moscow, Mumbai, Istanbul, Kuwait and Cannes. The company also manages distribution through subsidiaries in France, Germany, Italy, Austria, Spain, Russia, Singapore and the United States. While Chopard pursues its quest for international presence, Karl Friedrich maintains that the company will not give up its exclusivity.

"We definitely intend to stay true to our company's philosophy of creativity combined with quality craftsmanship, and increase the autonomy in production," explains Karl-Friedrich. "Last, but not least, we wish to further improve our service network and remain a family business."

LEFT Happy Sport ladies' watches in 18K rose gold, white gold and yellow gold, with ruby, sapphire and emerald cabochons.

CONCORD

*S*ince its inception in 1908, in Bienne, Switzerland, Concord has ranked among the world's most technologically advanced watchmakers. The company was founded by Walter E. Huguenin and Charles Bonny, two young Swiss watchmakers who shared an ambition to create watches of beautiful proportions by developing extremely thin movements which would not encumber design. The realization of this technological development afforded great artistic freedom to create mechanically precise and elegantly thin wrist-worn timepieces. These early achievements were a harbinger of many wonders to come, from Delirium, the thinnest watch in the world, to such one-of-a-kind creations as the Exor, a hand-crafted tourbillon timepiece of unsurpassed technical complication and mastery. Still driven by that same

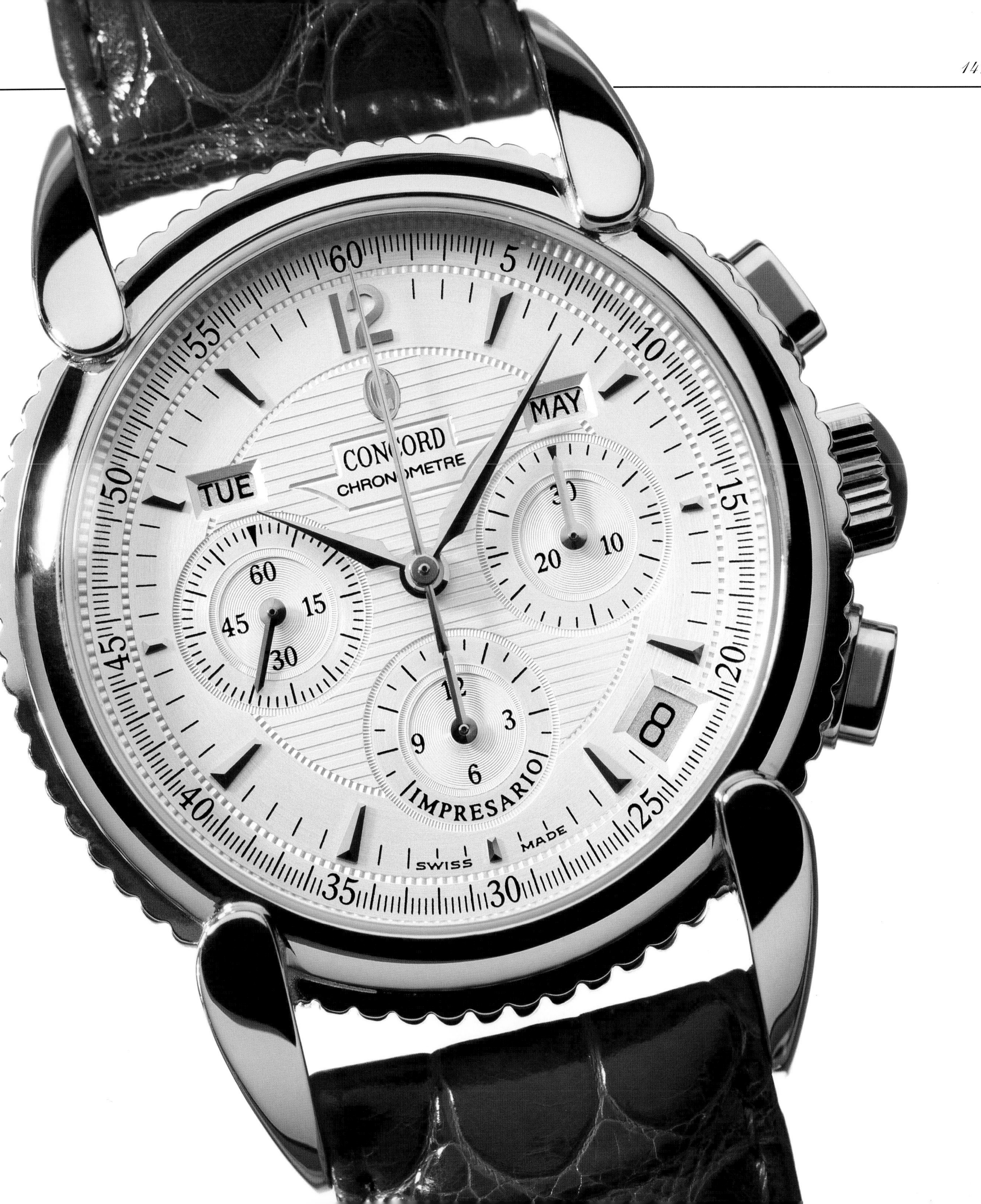
CONCORD
CHRONOMETRE
TUE
MAY
IMPRESARIO
SWISS MADE

inventive spirit almost a century later, Concord savors its reputation as an innovative designer and manufacturer of haute horlogerie and luxury timepieces distinguished by their technical virtuosity and design sophistication.

Concord established its dominance in wristwatch design early this century, just as wristwatches were gaining in popularity. The world's most prestigious jewelry houses including Tiffany & Co., Van Cleef & Arpels, and Cartier recognized Concord's excellence in engineering and design, and commissioned the young firm to develop private label watch lines. Concord also produced innovative stainless steel and gold-filled watches for the U.S. Army and Navy and for the general public. In the 1920s, Concord's prowess extended beyond wristwatches to the creation of the popular Ring Clock, the first portable travel alarm clock. After World War II, Concord's design leadership was evidenced in striking new designs for Concord's medallion and lidded wristwatches. The 1950s introduction of the covered bracelet watch for women was an instant success. It remains today a collector's item.

In 1979, Concord achieved a landmark in the history of watch design when it introduced Delirium, a timepiece measuring a mere 1.98 mm front to back, earning the industry's most sought appellation: "the thinnest watch in the world." Still in production today, the Delirium is also occasionally issued in limited edition commemorative series marked by distinctive dial designs.

OPENING PAGE Portrait of Walter E. Huguenin who with Charles Bonny and three other shareholders founded the Concord Watch Company in 1908.

PREVIOUS PAGE Impresario Chronographe on strap, in 18K rose gold, powered by a C.O.S.C.-certified automatic movement.

ABOVE Early this century, Concord designs were selected as private lines by Cartier and other world-famous jewelers.

ABOVE RIGHT The Saratoga Signature Collection. The Diamond and Sapphire pair seen here are in solid 18K white gold. His features 577 diamonds (17.19 cts) and 40 sapphires (2.34 cts.). Hers, 515 diamonds (8.79 cts.) and 32 sapphires (1.04 cts.).

FAR RIGHT Concord has produced pen watches and other handsomely crafted novelty timepieces for prestigious private labels, including Tiffany & Co.

BELOW Impresario Minute Repeaters. Each pair consists of a matching ladies' and gentlemen's model. Each timepiece is equipped with a minute-repeater mechanism that chimes the hours, quarter hours and minutes. Shown here the Platinum and Diamond pair.

Throughout the 1980s and 1990s, Concord earned an enviable reputation in the realm of haute horlogerie by unveiling a number of magnificently jeweled, one-of-a-kind timepieces of extraordinary complication: The Mariner Centenario series, the Exor and the Saratoga Splendours.

*I*ntroduced in 1997, the Saratoga Splendours is a spectacular quartet of one-of-a-kind timepieces inspired by — and named for — the beauty of cardinal gemstones: The Adamas (diamonds), The Rubeus (rubies), The Sapphirus (sapphires) and The Esmeraude (emeralds). Powered by mechani-

cal movements with complications such as a tourbillon regulating mechanism and minute repeater, each Splendour took more than a year to create. Each was crafted by hand in platinum and detailed by a crown set with a specially cut diamond, a superb crocodile leather strap, and

LEFT Delirium. In 1998, Delirium was issued in a special series commemorating the 90th Anniversary of Concord. These watches represent a consummate union of traditional Swiss craftsmanship and Chinese culture. The vividly pictorial dials are enameled by hand, and accentuated by diamonds and guilloché detail. The intricate workings of the superlative mechanical movements may be seen through the sapphire crystal centers of the casebacks which are engraved "Concord, 1908-1998" and "Limited Edition."

BELOW LEFT The Saratoga Splendours. This unprecedented quartet of one-of-a-kind platinum timepieces, unite technical virtuosity with the timeless intrigue of the world's most precious gemstones. **(LEFT TO RIGHT)** The Sapphirus, The Rubeus, The Esmeraude. Not shown: The Adamas.

BELOW Concord's current Delirium models are still elegantly slim, measuring less than 3mm.

elegant feuille hands. Successfully sold as a set, the Saratoga Splendours Collection is valued at three million Swiss francs.

In 1998, Concord presented another limited Saratoga series — the Signature Collection: haute joaillerie watches opulently adorned by diamonds, or in combinations of diamonds and fiery rubies or deep blue sapphires. These highly embellished wristwatches brilliantly reflect the signature of Concord craftsmanship. Each one bears the trademark of the individual master watchmaker who spent more than one year designing and hand crafting the timepiece.

The La Scala Diva Collection unites Concord's passion for precision and artistry in a sensuous symphony of style. Making their debut in the fall of 1998, these bold and beautiful timepieces feature new artistic dials that enhance the dramatic, cosmopolitan essence of La Scala. Each high-fashion Diva dial is radiantly detailed by a soleil-patterned mother-of-pearl inlay, coupled with pavé diamonds in distinctive geometric configurations.

This artistic and technical mastery is seen throughout Concord's watch collections, including the traditionally elegant Veneto collection, the geometric and grand La Scala family, and the exciting new Impresario line.

Dubbed "The new face of Concord," the Impresario Collection displays its particular har-

mony of art and engineering by uniting classic style with uncompromising technology and reliability. In design, each of these hand-crafted quartz and mechanical timepieces is defined by a distinctive coin-edge case with teardrop-shaped lugs. The coin-edge motif is repeated on the dial, crown and bracelet.

The exquisite one-of-a-kind Répétition Minutes are the crown jewels of the Impresario line. These six highly complicated mechanical masterworks are offered in three unique pairs, each comprised of a matching gentlemen's and ladies' model, the cases hand sculpted from precious platinum, platinum set with diamonds, or solid 18-karat rose gold. The hand-calibrated stem-winding movements are all equipped with a minute repeater that chimes the hours, quarter hours and minutes in soothing musical tones. In the three ladies' models, this sophisticated

ABOVE Inside the Impresario Chronographe is the world's first automatic chronograph movement that measures time to 1/10th of a second.

RIGHT La Scala Diva. The passionate beauty of Concord's successful La Scala luxury line takes center stage in the new La Scala Diva collection. Here, diamonds enhance the cool, dramatic appeal of solid 18K white gold. The dials feature soleil-patterned mother-of-pearl inlays and pavé diamonds.

mechanism represents a world premier — the extremely rare feature was once found only in much larger timepieces.

Premiering at the 1998 Basel Watch, Clock and Jewelry Fair, the Impresario Mechanique Collection, acclaimed for its powerful technical and aesthetic presence, marks the company's first major foray into the mechanical watch marketplace. The Collection includes four gentlemen's models of distinct complication in 18-karat rose gold or solid stainless steel.

*I*nside the Impresario Mechanique Chronographe is the world's first automatic chronograph movement that measures time to 1/10th-of-a-second and displays day of week, date and month. The manually wound Réserve de Marche boasts a 50-hour power reserve. The Impresario GMT (Greenwich Mean Time) features an automatic movement that enables the wearer to keep track of the time in two places. The Petite Seconde offers an ultra-thin automatic movement with a small seconds hand subdial at 6 o'clock, and a calendar window. Each of these precision movements required more than five years to develop. All four models are certified as meeting the official criteria of chronometer precision by the renowned c.o.s.c. (Swiss Official Control of Chronometers). Having passed fifteen days of rigorous precision testing, each individual Concord Impresario Mechanique timepiece is presented and packaged with its own c.o.s.c. certificate.

Other members of this newest leader line are the Impresario gentlemen's and ladies' quartz watches, expertly crafted in solid 18-karat yellow gold or solid stainless steel.

Today, design and distinction elevate Concord watch collections above the rest. From the extraordinary haute horlogerie marvels of the one-of-a-kind Saratoga Splendours, to the breathtaking beauty of the bejeweled Saratoga Signature Collection, to the impressive new Impresario family ... each of these Concord designs reflects a balance of artistry and technology, along with the exceptional craftsmanship and commitment that characterize every fine timepiece available from the House of Concord.

ABOVE Rounding out the new Impresario line are the attractively priced gentlemen's and ladies' quartz-powered bracelet and strap watches crafted in stainless steel. Reflecting an exciting innovation in watchmaking, the all-steel ladies' models are also available with diamond-set bezels.

LEFT Impresario Mechanique Collection. These Concord Impresario Réserve de Marche and Chronographe strap watches are hand-crafted of 18K rose gold. The inner workings of the sophisticated mechanical movements are revealed through sapphire crystal casebacks.

DANIEL ROTH

There is no mistaking a Daniel Roth watch — it is neither round, nor rectangular, nor oval. Instead, the case shape combines all three forms in a unique design that is instantly recognizable. The result of years of research and development defining and honing his personal style, the design of the case is symbolic of Daniel Roth's pursuit of his dreams. Before launching his watchmaking business in 1989, Roth made certain that everything was perfect down to the smallest detail of the watch design to the perfect location for his watchmaking factory in Le Sentier, in the Joux Valley close to the lake. The grandson of a watchmaker, Daniel Roth says his family history inspired his choice of profession. "In my family, when I was growing up, we talked about watchmaking and

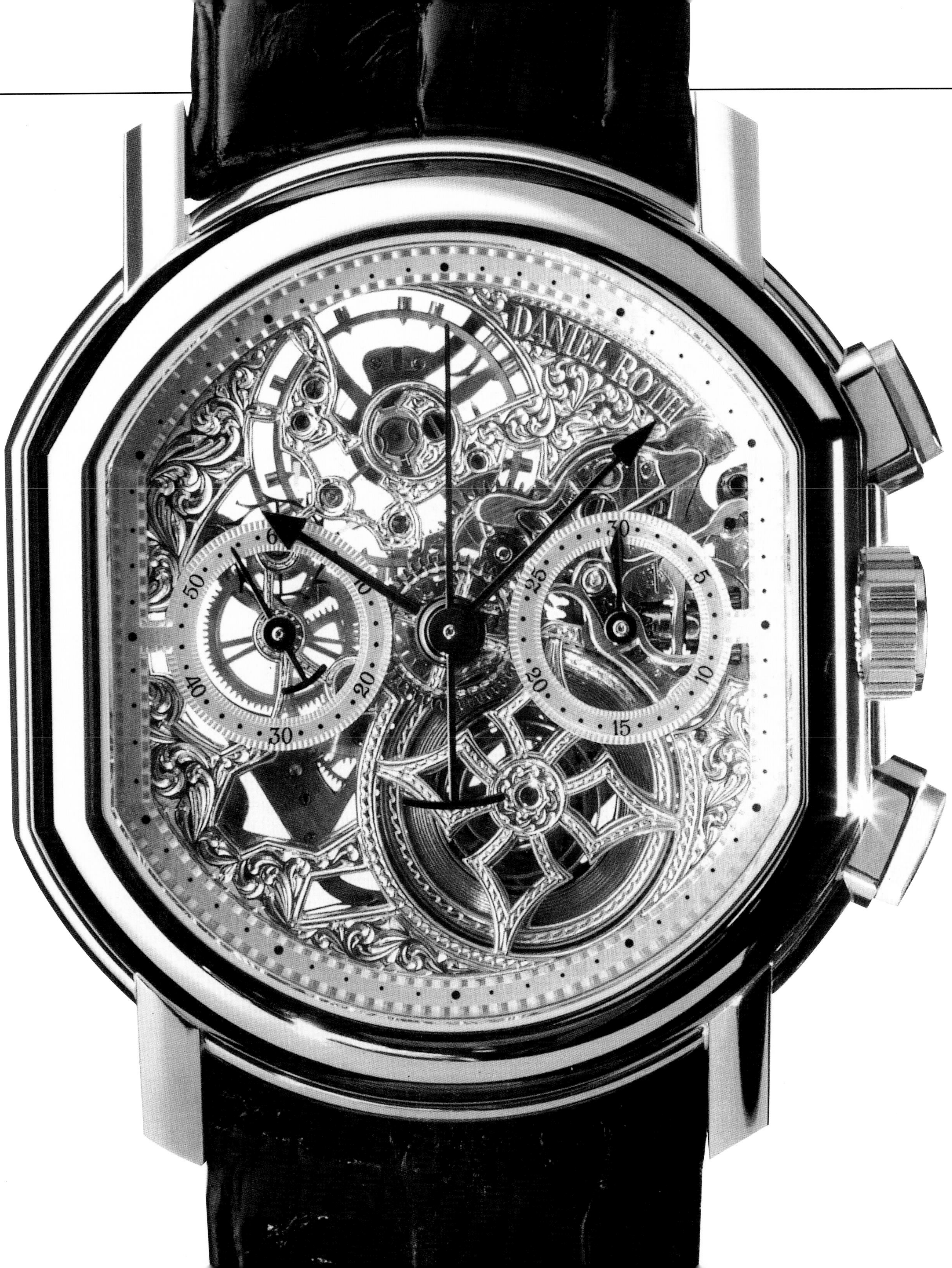
DANIEL ROTH

Switzerland. My grandfather had a small store where he sold and repaired watches himself. I was fascinated. He was very patient in introducing me to the profession he loved. He left me all of his old watchmaking tools, which I still treasure," Roth says.

When Daniel Roth was eighteen, he moved to Geneva and began working for leading watchmakers. As his reputation for his expertise began growing, the Chaumet Brothers tapped his talents to refurbish the collection of Abraham-Louis Breguet. Roth spent fourteen years studying the work of the master of watchmaking, and he redesigned Breguet's most important mechanism, the tourbillon, fitting it into a wristwatch. His skills earned him the position of head watchmaker, and during his ten years leading the craftsmen, Breguet was relaunched as a leading watchmaker.

Enriched with decades of experience and knowledge in watchmaking, Roth set out to launch his own line of

OPENING PAGE Portrait of Daniel Roth.

PREVIOUS PAGE Skeleton Chronograph in yellow gold contrasted by pink gold skeleton and white gold chapter rings. Two indicators reflect a 12-hour counter and minute indicator. Manual wind movement.

ABOVE Daniel Roth building, circa 1900 and the Daniel Roth Factory in 1997.

RIGHT The Double Face Tourbillon has brought international reknown and prestige to its highly talented creator. With the power reserve indicated on the caseback, it is the only Double Face Tourbillon in existence worldwide. This exceptional watch features a mechanical hand-wound movement and a 40-hour power reserve. The seconds are indicated on three superimposed graduated zones with three hands of different lengths.

TOP RIGHT Retrograde with ruthenium silvered dial, black crocodile strap.

CENTER RIGHT Perpetual Calendar.

BELOW RIGHT Minute Repeater with small second at six. Classic ruthenium silvered linear detail.

watches with one aim in mind: "My only ambition was to develop beautiful timepieces made according to watchmaking tradition," says Roth. While the first collection in 1989 numbered 300 timepieces, it has grown over the decade to nearly ten times that number.

*R*oth quickly became famed for his creations; today he is perhaps best known for his Double Face Tourbillon, a timepiece born of the knowledge Roth acquired at Breguet. Roth says that in developing the watch, he sought to create a tourbillon that could be worn everyday. The Double Face Tourbillon showcases the tourbillon on the face, while the reverse side displays the power reserve and the date.

One of his most recent complications is the Instantaneous Perpetual Calendar, in which the day, month and year are constructed as jumping mechanisms. Instead of changing slowly over time, the day quickly changes at midnight. At midnight at the end of the year, all three numbers jump at once. The complication requires that the day, date, year and leap year are on three different dials, demanding absolute perfection in crafting

the timepiece. The automatic timepiece features a skeleton dial.

In 1998, he celebrated his tenth anniversary with the release of the "Papillon" complicated timepiece, a horological innovation that Roth has patented. A compelling timepiece, the "Papillon" is distinguished by its unusual minute hand which is actually two hands that take turns showing themselves around a horseshoe-shaped dial, creating the illusion that one hand is magically crossing to the other side of the dial. Technically speaking, the hands are mounted on opposite sides of a centrally located disc. As the disc rotates, one hand remains hidden while the other counts the minutes from zero to 60. The moment the first hand reaches 60 it disappears, and at precisely the same time, the second hand emerges at zero.

What should be made clear is that Roth himself does not know, at the outset, whether or not some of the mechanical wonders he dreams up can actually be executed. While this is a consideration that would intimidate others, the unknown intrigues Roth. "There is always an exciting period before being certain that technology can carry out what I have imagined," Roth says.

While he is regarded foremost as a master of complications, Daniel Roth's collection includes fashionable sports watches and ladies' jeweled watches. In 1994, the watchmaker launched a chronograph timepiece, followed a year later by the Sports Series of automatic watches now available with a rugged, yet stylish, metal bracelet and featuring boldly colored

faces in bright yellow and red.

To meet the particular needs of women more concerned with beauty and fashion than with the mechanical workings of a watch, Daniel Roth in 1996 introduced the Boutique Line of fine watches. The styles range from very colorful, sportswear inspired designs to elaborately adorned jeweled watches that boast diamonds, rubies and sapphires. Most recently, Roth introduced a steel watch with diamonds, and all of the timepieces are available with automatic or quartz movements.

The consumate watchmaker, Roth continues to explore the art of design. A recent high-jewelry watch in the Lady Automatic series combines the warmth of coral with baguette-cut diamonds, set off by a crocodile band. In keeping with Roth's dedication to creating the finest watches available, these timepieces are also available with Roth's exceptional automatic movements.

*B*orn into the tradition of watchmaking, and having experienced the traditions of centuries of watchmaking at Breguet, Roth enjoys a special place in the history of horology. He says that although he is respectful of the strides made in technology, he feels that the watchmaking industry is the same today as it has always been — new watchmakers continue to establish small workshops dedicated to the pursuit of precision watchmaking. For Roth, horology holds special charm.

"I find the mechanics of timepieces more and more intriguing. It encour- ages us to learn more and more, to push beyond our limitations until finally, it becomes a game. Capturing time in a little box, adorning it with a technical and artistic design... this seems magical to me."

ABOVE Stainless steel sports bracelet, automatic.

LEFT GMT Collection. Gents or Mid-Size with linear or lacquer dial.

GERALD GENTA

To behold a watch from Gerald Genta is to view time from a whole new perspective. No longer are sweeping hands strictly relied upon to tell the hour or windows used to reveal dates. If there is a more inventive and aesthetic approach, Gerald Genta will offer his exploration. Consider the Grande Sonnerie and its step-like structured bezel of eight successive reeds. Narrowing to the top much like a Mayan Pyramid, the case shape suggests the knowledge and skill housed inside the timepiece required to perform its myriad functions. Or take a glance at the Retro, a world premier: the watch single-handedly makes the time apparent. Details are often an obsession for watchmakers and ultimately they are the gauge for discerning one timepiece from another. And Gerald Genta is a master of details — from his unusual

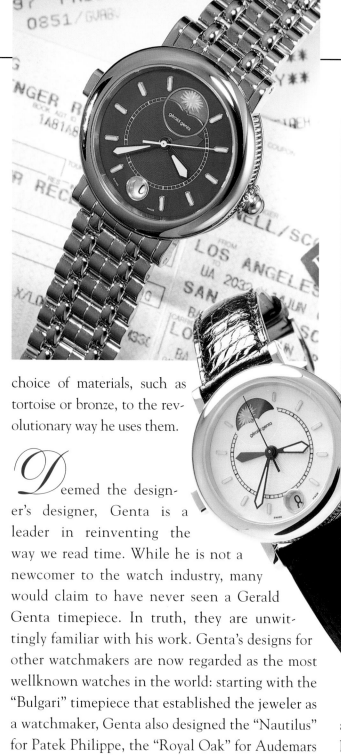

choice of materials, such as tortoise or bronze, to the revolutionary way he uses them.

Deemed the designer's designer, Genta is a leader in reinventing the way we read time. While he is not a newcomer to the watch industry, many would claim to have never seen a Gerald Genta timepiece. In truth, they are unwittingly familiar with his work. Genta's designs for other watchmakers are now regarded as the most wellknown watches in the world: starting with the "Bulgari" timepiece that established the jeweler as a watchmaker, Genta also designed the "Nautilus" for Patek Philippe, the "Royal Oak" for Audemars Piguet, the "Constellation" and "Seamaster" for Omega and IWC's "Ingenieur" model.

Living in Switzerland and possessing a deep appreciation for art and fashion, Genta naturally began designing for watchmakers. Throughout the 1960s, he created the landmark designs for the leading watchmakers, but he also produced many pieces for collectors whose demands for complicated timepieces inspired him

to launch his own watchmaking company in 1969.

Today, his unique sensibility of matching art and science is almost certainly enhanced by a duality in the creation process — Genta explores each design concept from his headquarters in the fashionable, luxurious landscape of Monte Carlo before having them executed in the heartland of watchmaking, La Brassus, Switzerland. "I am working in a tight collaboration with a master watchmaker who brings his know how. The result is an osmosis between design and technology which makes the Gerald Genta watches so special," says Genta.

There is certainly a great deal of useful whimsy involved in Genta's creations. On the face of the Backtimer, for example, are three windows that count down the days until the new

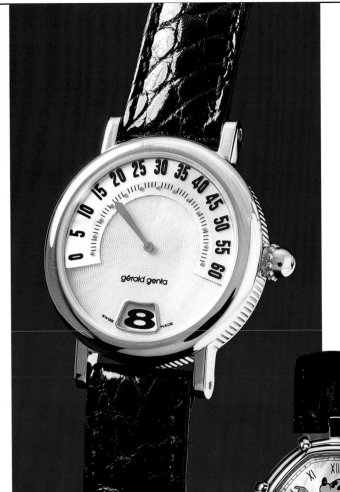

place the wearer is visiting, and can be tucked away under the hour hand when it is not needed. The Day-Night perfectly exhibits Genta's commitment toward producing lifestyle watches that help the wearer make the most of every moment. Genta's most celebrated timepiece, the Retro, is inspired by the digital watches of the '70s which "revolutionized the way of reading the time," says Genta. "Since then, there has never been any innovation of this sense. Therefore, I have invented a special way of reading time that is a link between tradition and modernity." It's no wonder that the Retro, unveiled in 1990, exhibits a youthful and fashionable dynamism. The Retro is patented for its ingenious system of jumping hours and retrograde minutes. The minute hand travels 210 degrees before returning to its starting point with each hour change.

The Bi-Retro is an extension of the Retro that includes the date, and the Retro concept becomes all the more delightful in the Fantasy line, with its animated characters flashing across mother-of-pearl faces. No taboos seem to exist for Genta, who

millennium. Afterward, the wearer can reset the countdown as a reminder for other impending events, such as an anniversary or birthday.

In our faster paced world that sees increasing global travel, Genta reveals another contemporary and practical timepiece, the Day-Night watch that reveals two time zones. Highly acclaimed, its face features a window revealing the sun and the moon in the time zone the wearer has just left, so with a quick glance, the wearer immediately knows whether it is day or night in his hometown, and whether he'll be disturbing his family with a late night phone call, or catching the answering machine at the office. A third hand on the watch is set to match the local time of the

FAR LEFT Retro Classic, reinventing time. This watch with its "jump hours and retrograde minutes" defies the principle of telling the time with two hands.

ABOVE Retro Fantasy.

CENTER Fantasy.

LEFT Ladies' Retro. The Retro classic made for ladies using the ease of the quartz movement. This watch is available with diamond bezel, even in stainless steel.

ABOVE Bi-Retro. In redefining the wristwatch, the Bi-Retro incorporates an ingenious automatic movement with jumping hours and retrograde minutes combined with a retrograde hand calendar.

ABOVE AND OVAL Grand Sonnerie.

RIGHT Tourbillon. Newly designed Retro case featuring a crystal fibre dial and tourbillon escapement at the 6 o'clock position.

FAR RIGHT Gefica Chrono. The high-end sports watch in stainless steel with chronograph movement, day and date.

determined long ago the need for a quartz watch for those who are not intrigued with the dazzling mechanical watches; for this reason, the Retro, Bi-Retro and Fantasy watches, as well as other collections, are available in quartz.

One of Genta's more intriguing timepieces, not only for the story of its creation, is the Gefica Safari watch, developed upon special request. "I designed the watch for three friends who decided to go on a safari in Africa. They needed a watch that wouldn't be shiny or reflect the sun in order to keep from frightening the animals while hunting. This inspired me to create this very original watch, in bronze."

Unusual as the first watch to feature a bronze case, the Gefica is also one of the first watches to include a compass. Drawing from the elements of nature that inspired the Gefica, Genta experimented with tortoise, slate and malachite in the design. Many variations in the style are now available, including a chronograph, perpetual calendar and dual time zone. In 1991, Genta marked the 700th anniversary of the foundation of the Swiss Confederation with a commemorative timepiece brandishing the red and white colors of the Swiss flag on a mother-of-pearl

when mechanical time-pieces are incredibly popular. It is fitting, because it is a momentum sparked when he set out on his own, with a mission to translate the artistry of watchmaking through his dynamic designs.

True to his passion to create the most technically precise and aesthetically beautiful timepieces, Genta continues to produce profound complications that are hallmarked by the Geneva Seal. But further attesting to his visionary spirit, Gerald Genta is celebrating his twentieth year crafting watches under his own name at a time

ABOVE Gefica Power Reserve. Bold, inventive embodiment of technical prowess. The window displaying the power reserve is reminiscent of vintage auto gauges.

FAR LEFT Perpetual Calendar. This watch incorporates dials of various colors and combinations, using mother-of-pearl sub-dials and lapis lazuli moon phase. Phosphorescent hour markers and hands make the time easy to read at all hours.

LEFT Gefica Chrono. High-end sports watch, in bronze.

GIRARD PERREGAUX

A watchmaker for more than 200 years, Girard-Perregaux has built an enduring legacy in the most demanding of luxury industries. Renowned for their exacting standards and their adamant refusal to compromise on any aspect of the watchmaking process, the Swiss firm has seduced the most prestigious names in the world, from connoisseurs to elite companies, such as Ferrari. The Italian car manufacturer collaborated with Girard-Perregaux in 1994 to produce a limited edition "Tribute to Ferrari" series. And in 1995, a full line of "For Ferrari" watches — complete with the famous stallion emblem — was unveiled. The company refers to itself as a "manufactory," emphasizing the fact that Girard-Perregaux is solely responsible for each and every step of a watch's journey, from inception to final production.

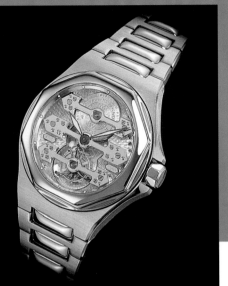

OPENING PAGE The Villa Marguerite, the public museum of the Girard-Perregaux foundation, opened in the spring of 1999. The museum is dedicated to the preservation of watchmaking skills and horlogerie.

PREVIOUS PAGE Girard Perregaux Laureato Sport Tourbillon with Three Gold Bridges comes in the sporty Laureato case in stainless steel or on request, in yellow, rose or white gold. The highly recognizable trademark movement with its wide, solid bridges can be admired through the sapphire crystal.

ABOVE Laureato Sport Tourbillon with Three Gold Bridges.

ABOVE CENTER Girard Perregaux presents the Tourbillon with Three Gold Bridges, with the smallest ever movement of 27mm. Fine mechanical timepieces have not traditionally been associated the feminine wrist. Girard-Perregaux, however, is dedicating this Haute Horlogerie creation to women, who are increasingly attracted to technically sophisticated watches. This model can be set with brilliants or other precious stones.

ABOVE RIGHT Single Bridge tourbillon with power reserve.

CENTER OVAL Three Gold Bridges tourbillon skeleton.

RIGHT OVAL Vintage 1997 split-second chronograph modeled from Girard-Perregaux's 1960 model

Unlike other noted brands, Girard-Perregaux manufactures and assembles their own timepieces. The firm boasts three separate factories in La Chaux-de-Fonds, Switzerland, one for movement-making, another for case-making and the last for watch assembly.

La Chaux-de-Fonds has been a hub for elite watchmaking since the middle of the 18th century, but Girard-Perregaux's own history first began in Geneva in 1791. At this time, J.F. Bautte founded a watchmaking studio in his own name in the capital of French-speaking Switzerland. A gifted innovator, he explored the many realms of watchmaking and devised a method for producing extremely thin timepieces. With a burgeoning reputation, the firm passed into the hands of Constant Girard in the mid-1800s. And when Girard married Marie Perregaux in 1854, the legendary moniker of Girard-Perregaux was born.

In 1867, after intensive research on the use of gold in a movement, Girard-Perregaux created a masterpiece: the famous Tourbillon with Three Gold Bridges. The tourbillon watch is a technological marvel, whose goal is to correct the inaccuracies a timepiece is subjected to by the negative effects of gravity. The triple-gold-bridge model unveiled by Girard-Perregaux was an immediate triumph. At the Paris Universal Exhibitions of 1867 and 1889, the watch was an obvious selection for a gold medal. And, in the ultimate show of respect, organizers of the 1901 exhibition judged the watch too perfect to compete.

In 1981, 20 replicas of the original tourbillon pocket watch with three gold bridges were issued by Girard-Perregaux, underscoring the fact that its watchmakers were still masters of the technical know-how needed to execute such complicated works. Each watch required a six- to eight-month production calendar, with most of the labor dedicated solely to the arduous process of assembling and adjusting the intricate components.

In celebration of its bicentennial in 1991, Girard-Perregaux adapted its three-gold-bridged tourbillon to a wristwatch format for the first time. Capitalizing on the world's fascination with the exquisite timepiece, Girard-Perregaux introduced a revolutionary wristwatch with a one-bridge tourbillon mechanism fitted into a "tonneau"-shaped case in 1996. And in 1997, Girard-Perregaux's tireless craftsmen once again surpassed all expectations when they created a "tonneau"-shaped tourbillon mechanism with three bridges. Produced in a very limited and numbered series, Girard-Perregaux's latest marvel is already considered the crown of several distinguished private collections.

Girard-Perregaux assures the exquisite quality of each of its creations by producing just 15,000 timepieces a year. 10,000 of these boast the company's own name, while the remaining 5,000 are emblazoned with the distinctive "Pour Ferrari" seal.

Luigi Macaluso, the present-day owner of Girard-Perregaux, fostered a relationship with Ferrari nearly three decades ago. A professional driver for the Fiat group in the 1970s, Macaluso is a long-time friend and associate of Ferrari's president, Luca Cordera. When Macaluso purchased Girard-Perregaux in 1992 he became the first Italian CEO of a Swiss watchmaking company and a

TOP Ferrari Formula 1 stopwatch.

ABOVE Girard-Perregaux pour Ferrari F-300 Chronograph and the Lady F (Femme automatic with date). The F300 is the newest of the Girard-Perregaux pour Ferrari chronographs. For its new line of dials of the now famous line of watches, the manufactory has again used carbon fibre, but in a more classic version, and with a choice of ivory, black, or black with silvered counters. Because it is the dial that endows a watch with much of its character, Girard-Perregaux has paid meticulous attention to every detail, emlazoning each dial with F300, the hallmark for 1998.

BELOW AND BOTTOM Lady F, Lady F jewelry. Sporty and robust with a strong Girard-Perregaux identity, the new model in the ladies' collection is simply called F, for Femme (Woman). A feminine version of the "Girard-Perregaux pour Ferrari" model, the watch boasts soft, generously rounded lines, its case harmonizes with a supple bracelet of classic links in original combinations of gold and steel. Fitted with an automatic mechanical movement and a cambered sapphire crystal. The screw-down back and crown guarantee total water-resistance to 50 meters. With the small rearing horse emblem adorning a selection of dials in the famous Italian car-maker's colors, the "F" fits perfectly into the exclusive "Pour Ferrari" line.

FACING PAGE, RIGHT Richeville automatic chronograph.

BELOW Vintage 1945 gents' automatic and ladies' watches. Quartz.

collaboration with Ferrari seemed natural. "Because Ferrari is a dream car that is unique to the world, we decided to create something that was for the top collectors," Macaluso said. He signed a co-branding deal with Cordera and directed his company in the production of an exclusive "For Ferrari" line of "limited-edition timepieces in which what was inside the watch counted just as much as the design," according to Macaluso.

The first generation of Ferrari-inspired watches appeared in 1994, and culminated in 1995 when Girard-Perregaux showcased a one-of-a-kind timepiece adorned with a fabulous Ferrari stallion insignia carved out of ruby. This exquisite collector's watch quickly sold for $150,000.

In 1997 the Ferrari motor company commemorated its 50th year by issuing the fabulous F50, the type of remarkable vehicle that could only exist twice in a century. To share in the celebration, Girard-Perregaux once again joined forces with the Italian automotive legend and created the F50 wristwatch.

Girard-Perregaux chose gold, platinum or titanium for the "chassis," which contains the F50

watch's complex mechanism. Masterfully crafted, the F50 timepiece is a colossal technical feat. It boasts an automatic chronograph with a perpetual calendar, capable of correcting the date, even in leap years, until the dawn of the 22nd century.

*G*irard-Perregaux issued the Ferrari F50 watch in two very limited series. The first series of 349 was designed for the 349 owners of Ferrari F50 cars. Owners who acquired the F50 watch were cordially invited by Girard-Perregaux to have their names and the serial number of their automobile engraved on the watch's case. A second series of 250 chronographs was then offered to distinguished collectors.

A consummate watchmaker, Girard-Perregaux cannot be categorized solely as a manufac-

ABOVE RIGHT A Grand Classic, Girard-Perregaux's Traveler II features an automatic movement with an alarm function, second time zone and date window.

CENTER RIGHT Classique automatic, featuring the Girard-Perregaux 3100 movement.

BELOW Commemorating the 1957 Testa Rossa, the GP 250 TR is limited to 2,000 pieces, a 24-hour automatic chronograph with sub-dial and counters.

FAR LEFT Vintage 1945 gents' automatic.

LEFT Girard-Perregaux Pour Ferrari chronograph.

BELOW Tourbillon chronograph in 18K gold with Three Gold Bridges.

turer of grand complications such as the tourbillon mechanism or as a refined collaborator with the likes of Ferrari. They also produce hand-winding and automatic mechanical movements, and an estimated seven percent of their line holds quartz movements. World renowned for their strict parameters on quality control, Girard-Perregaux ships 50,000 sophisticated movements a year to other prestigious watchmaking brands.

As Luigi Macaluso says of his company, "When you buy a Girard-Perregaux watch, you are buying a piece of a dream, a piece of aesthetics, and finally, of course, a functional item for the telling of time."

HAMILTON

The evolution of America's great watch brand is a story of constant technical innovation and striking leaps of styling inspiration. From its beginnings as a small watch manufacturer in Lancaster, Pennsylvania in 1892, Hamilton has grown to become the most well known American watch brand and, more importantly, America's timekeeper for more than 100 years. Hamilton first made its mark during an era of rapid growth in the railroad industry and a consequent rise in tragic railroad crashes. The train wrecks which had become common in the late 1800s were often due to innaccurate timekeeping—leading to the widespread imposition of stricter standards for railroad watches. Hamilton produced a series of pocket watches that surpassed even these new standards, establishing for the brandname

a reputation as the "watch of railroad accuracy." The best-selling Broadway Limited, considered a technical marvel in its day, featured 21 extra-fine rubies in gold settings, a patent motor barrel adjusted to temperature, double roller escapement, steel escape wheel, Breguet hairspring, compensation balance, patent micrometric regulator and elegant damaskeening.

Hamilton's commitment to superior product standards and technological progress earned the company an unmatched reputation for accuracy and dependability among professionals in a number of industries. In the 1930s, Hamilton took to the skies when United Airlines, TWA, Eastern and Northwest airlines all adopted the brand as their official timepiece.

Throughout the twentieth century, Hamilton has spanned the globe as the watch of choice of scientists, explorers and the US military. Hamilton timepieces have traveled with Admiral Byrd to the North and South Poles and to the outer reaches of the earth's atmosphere with the

Picards, who made the first successful balloon flight into the stratosphere. Hamilton watches have also ascended Mt. Everest, traversed the Great Gobi Desert of Mongolia with Roy Chapman Andrews in 1927 and served on the fields of battle during the First and Second World Wars and the Korean War.

As mass production began to replace the less efficient guild system that had long reigned in Europe, Hamilton led the way in developing effective and reliable mass production methods. Hamilton's successes, together with the quality of their products, drew the attention of Switzer-

OPENING PAGE The Original Hamilton Watch Company, located in Lancaster, Pennsylvania, is now placed on the "National Register of Historic Places" by the US Dept. of Interior.

PREVIOUS PAGE Khaki Chronograph.

TOP Odysee, 1969, inspired by the Stanley Kubrick film, Space Odyssey 2001, stainless steel, movement grade G. 642.

ABOVE Thor II, 1963, 10K gold-plated, G. 686.

TOP RIGHT Meteor, 1961, 505 Electric, 10K gold-filled.

BOTTOM LEFT Lloyd, 1955, 10K gold-filled, G. 754 & 770.

BOTTOM RIGHT Meadowbrook, 1933, G. 979 and 878.

land's master watchmakers. European experts put the mass-produced Hamilton movements to the test and found them to be as accurate and dependable as their own.

$\mathcal{H}$amilton continued to impress its European competitors with a series of other innovations. In 1957 the world's first electric watch, the Ventura, was introduced. The electric movement replaced both the mainspring and winding stem with a battery power source. The electric current set the balance in motion and the hairspring regulated its oscillations. This revolutionary innovation was followed by Hamilton's introduction in 1970 of the first electronic digital watch, the Pulsar, futuristically billed as "a solid state wrist computer programmed to tell time."

Apart from its many technological innovations, Hamilton also drew acclaim for its design and styling concepts. Hamilton played a crucial role in identifying the importance of the female market, beginning with the 1908 O-size, completely cased pendant watch named the "Lady Hamilton."

In the early 1900s, styling began to take on greater importance in watch design and Hamilton began to make increasingly elegant and beautiful timepieces, as seen in the 1930 designs of the Ardmore, the Contour and the Sutton. The glamorous styling of the Diamond Index, for example, was equal to the work of the most renowned watchmakers of the time: Patek Philippe, Audemars Piguet and Rolex. Hamilton was the first to develop sophisticated new alternatives to the traditional round watch, and, today, unique case shapes are a Hamilton signature.

LEFT Victor II, 1961, 505 Electric, 10K gold-filled.

CENTER K475, 1960, an automatic styled after the electric timepieces, G. 690.

BELOW LEFT Chatham, 1955, 14K gold, S12/0 (size of the movement).

BELOW Ventura, 1957, the first battery powered watch.

BOTTOM (TOP TO BOTTOM) A Hamilton testimonial ad circa 1911 about the watch whose precision is credited with helping eliminate train collisions: Graduation Ad Campaign, circa 1941.

Hamilton reached a pinnacle of innovative styling with the introduction of the Ventura and two other lines in the 1950s. As Don Sauers wrote in Time for America, "Hamilton's advanced styling . . . with the Ventura with its shield-shaped case and two-tone strap; the eccentric, off-center Victor; and the asymmetrical, oval-cased Spectra was . . . startling. They shattered preconceived notions and defied sacred cows."

The Hamilton reputation for fashionable design drew some of Hollywood's biggest names. Elvis Presley showed off his Ventura in 1961's Blue Hawaii. Stanley Kubrick commissioned Hamilton to design a special watch for his epochal 2001: A Space Odyssey. Recently, the Ventura has made a comeback, appearing in the 1997 hit Men in Black and 1998's Lethal Weapon 4. Today, Hamilton continues its creative tradition of ground-breaking timepieces by combining pure watchmaking mastery with an eye for sheer aesthetic pleasure. Two new lines inspired by the timepieces of yesteryear demonstrate Hamilton's uninterrupted command of the watchmaking craft: the American Classics and the Khaki collections.

The American Classics feature the very finest in craftsmanship and artistry. Born of the same attention to detailing that was the hallmark of Hamilton design in the 1930s, the new Chatham and Contour capture the spirit of women today.

Hamilton now offers bracelet straps in many designs, all of which enhance the vintage look. Hamilton timepieces currently feature unparalleled detailing of the dial, a variety of

watchfaces, cases and straps and the masterful use of color. The new Hamilton Classics are eye-catching, contemporary pieces that speak volumes about the wearer. The Chatham's hourglass shape mirrors the curves of a woman. The crystal adds depth and dimension; the stylized lugs and markers provide a distinct character. The luminous white case further enhances markers that are set off against a peach background, striking a balance between the watch's vibrant styling and soft color. Each watch has an individual character that complements the personality, lifestyle and spirit of the contemporary woman.

Part of the American Classics line, the Lloyd has become very popular with both male and female consumers. The defining rectangular shape and stylized cornices of the original 1955 Lloyd return in an updated design that gracefully harmonizes vintage style with modernity.

Hamilton offers the simple yet striking design of the new Hamilton Khaki to both men and women as well. A direct descendant of the timepieces created by the company for the US military in World War II, the current collection ranges from sports watches to military-themed watches featuring Swiss quartz, automatic or hand-wound movements, bracelet or leather strap and a clean-cut, versatile look. The new Khaki collection incorporates all of the qualities of the current line into a stronger, bolder, more active timepiece.

Twelve new Khaki watches — sleek, technically advanced and fashion-forward — feature all of the sport watch functions one could desire in an action accessory. The bold white numbers, red minute markers and red sweeping second hand accentuate the black dial while the brown, genuine leather strap or the new integrated Delrin by Dupont and stainless steel bracelet enhance the pure, rugged sportiness of the watch.

The new series will feature several styles in quartz, as well as automatic or chronograph models, with sapphire crystal and an innovative crown protection lever that flips down over the crown for use during the most extreme undertakings. Active men and women may choose between two different case sizes to perfectly match any on-the-go lifestyle. With the integration of new materials in the bracelet and bold coloring on the dial, the ruggedly designed new Hamilton will again establish the watchmaker as a leader in the development of sophisticated new products.

*T*oday is the dawn of a new era for the brand. The relaunch of Hamilton, which began in 1998, includes the introduction of twenty new and rejuvenated watches along with an exciting new approach to advertising, packaging and displays. The eye-catching new marketing campaign contrasts the routine nature of most watch advertising with a fresh look geared to attract younger consumers, taking watch advertising to new levels.

Despite this new energy and style, however, Hamilton is committed to the tradtions of the American spirit in which it was born. Marrying its heritage of classic styling to a mastery of the ongoing changes in technology and fashion, Hamilton will continue to be a leader in product innovation and design and a creator of peerless dependability and accuracy. Hamilton: Born in the USA.

ABOVE Lloyd.

TOP LEFT Auto 40mm Chronograph.

BOTTOM LEFT
The Hamilton watches that served as the official timekeepers of Admiral Byrd's Antarctic Expeditions in 1928.

CENTER LEFT Ryan, 1952, 10K gold-filled, G. 752 and 770.

HUBLOT

*P*ossibly the greatest risk ever taken in the advancement of the wristwatch was when Carlo Crocco replaced leather straps and gold bracelets with a natural rubber strap, creating his timepiece known as the Hublot. The concept of the strap is a bold departure from convention, as is the complex construction and intricate design of the case, resulting in a timepiece that is decades ahead of its time. It is a status affirmed by those who can afford any luxury and choose the Hublot, adding to its reputation as the watch of royalty. "Everyone has a preconceived notion of what a watch is. This is what a watch should be," says Ed Suhyda, Regional Manager for Hublot. Sensible and elegant, the natural rubber strap is at first puzzling to connoisseurs of fine timepieces who are accustomed to gold, leather or platinum. But as Suhyda

points out, a masterpiece is not to be tossed into a closet, drawer or security box. It should be worn every day and the Hublot — with its sleek, practical strap — is unique as the only timepiece that travels seamlessly from the depths of the sea to the executive club. It is the timepiece for the discriminating person who possesses a zeal for living life to the fullest.

"Hublot is undoubtedly the most sensual watch in the world. It is easily worn with a bathing suit at the beach, then moves gracefully into

evening with the latest fashions from Prada, Escada, St. John, Armani or Chanel. Hublot never detracts from an outfit, whereas a metal bracelet hangs out like a sore thumb. Hublot is a signature to anything you wear," says Suhyda. "It allows you

to enjoy your life. If you want to hike, bike, fish, swim or ski, you never need to take the watch off, the strap endures through all activities."

The timepiece is the result of Carlo Crocco's consuming mission to design one watch to perfection. In fact, he was so relentless in his belief in the perfect watch that the first Hublot, black face and black strap, endured for eight years as the only version available. Only recently has he begun to explore the use of white and vibrant blue and green on the watchface. "The idea was to create a style and not constantly change it. Admittedly, the most skeptical of watch wearers begins to appreciate the beauty of Hublot once it is on the wrist. After all, it was made for the body, not the showcase," explains Crocco.

As a child, Crocco watched curiously as his family designed scores of beautiful timepieces. In fact, the prolific rate of creation was troubling. As he saw watchcase after watchcase produced to keep up with customer demand for new models, he began questioning the logic of a designer out-moding himself each year. Determined, he vowed to create the perfect watch, with no detail over-looked. The case, the timekeeping system, the strap — every element would have to be perfect. "It was important to present the complete con-cept when the timepiece would be released. We came with something completely new. It was not

ABOVE Chronograph gents' model in 18K gold with mechanical functions. Quartz movement with two independant motors. Water-resistant to 50 meters.

CENTER Chronograph gents' model in 18K white gold set with princess cut diamonds. Water-resistant to 50 meters, self-winding mechanical movement.

LEFT Chronograph gents' model in steel with mechanical functions. Quartz movement with two independant motors. Water-resistant to 50 meters.

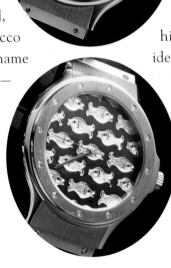

a test. It was the launching of a brand," explains Crocco, who invested four years and more than a million dollars before his passion for the perfect timepiece became a reality.

From the start, he decided on the porthole shape of the case, from which the Hublot derives its name. On a train between Geneva and Zurich, the name was established during a conversation with French travel companions who looked at the shape of the watch and declared, "hublot," meaning "porthole." Crocco liked the sound of it and the name stayed. Intricate as the case is — finished by hand in 250 steps to incorporate a stunning combination of matte and shiny surface — the strap posed a greater puzzle during the developmental process.

A seemingly easy concept to realize, this singular task of creating a strap proved elusive. First, Crocco recognized that leather bands, a perfect complement to the watchface, deteriorate with age and take hours to dry once they become wet. On the other hand, his sketches of metal bands were disappointing as the bands appeared too obtrusive for the refined look he desired.

In 1977, during a brainstorming session with associates, Crocco made a crucial breakthrough. When his graphic designer began sketching ideas for straps, he completely blackened in the strap. Struck by how well the black complemented his timepiece without overwhelming the design, Crocco knew he had found the elegant and refined look he wanted. He surmised that the strap might possibly be developed from rubber. "The problem was that we wanted to have pure rubber, so it's natural, and at the same time it had to be durable. The trick is, creating a natural rubber is easy, creating a durable rubber is easy, but creating a strap that incorporates both is difficult," Crocco explains. "We also wanted to provide every size of strap without having to cut the straps to fit. So we measured the different wrists in all the parts of the world from Japan to America to develop the different sizes — to the millimeter." Further, the straps were tested with everything from cologne to salt water, perfume, ammonia, cleansers and detergents to ensure that nothing would harm the strap.

Finally, Crocco unveiled his Hublot at the Basel Jewelry and Watch Fair in 1980. While it has taken almost twenty years for the rest of the watchmaking world to catch on — only recently have other leading watchmakers begun to use rubber straps on their timepieces — distinguished connoisseurs immediately recognized the superior qualities of the Hublot. In particular, King Constantine of

ABOVE King and Queen of Sweden. The King wears a Hublot.

LEFT "Teddy Bear" limited edition ladies' models. 18K gold set with diamonds, sapphires, rubies and emeralds on enameled motif. Quartz movement, water-resistant to 50 meters.

BELOW (left) Limited edition gents' models in 18K yellow or rose gold, with self-winding mechanical movement, water-resistant to 50 meters. (left to right) "Wild Horses;" "Polo Player" set with diamonds, enameled dial set with diamonds and rubies; "Wild Horses" with enameled dial; and "Peacock" set with diamonds and emeralds on the bezel, enameled dial set with diamonds and rubies.

TOP Ladies jewelry watches in 18K gold, with diamonds on the bezel, endpieces, clasp, on hour markers or dial paved with diamonds. gents' model with the bezel, clasp and endpieces set with diamonds.

TOP CENTER Elegant automatic, steel case set with 48 diamonds on the bezel and 36 on the endpieces, self-winding mechanical movement, water-resistant to 50 meters.

TOP RIGHT Giorgio Armani, seen wearing a Hublot.

RIGHT Classic gents' model steel and gold and medium model in steel and gold. Quartz movement. Water-resistant to 50 meters.

Greece who is known for his impeccable taste — his opinions in matters of style and elegance are often considered the last word. On a trip to Switzerland in the early 80s, he found himself fascinated with the unusual watch, not only for its porthole face, but for its simple black rubber strap. Intrigued, His Majesty bought one. More than pleased with it, he grew so fond of the comfortable and stylish timepiece that he bought one for King Juan Carlos of Spain. In no time, the Hublot was seen on the wrists of all of Europe's elite.

"The people who wear Hublot don't care if you know what they're wearing, they're self-made individuals, they're leaders," Suhyda says. "You don't buy an Hublot to impress someone else. You buy an Hublot to impress yourself. And when you buy things to impress yourself, you do everything better than everyone else and everyone is impressed with you. That's the kind of person that wears an Hublot."

*A*vailable in five sizes in gold, platinum, steel and various metal combinations with or without diamonds, the timepieces come in two variations of the porthole style: Elegance and Classic. The bezel of the Classic timepiece is marked with screws indicating the hour, while the Elegance line features a slightly curved bezel with hour markers on the face. Each movement powering the Hublot is the finest made in Switzerland, whether it is the automatic move-

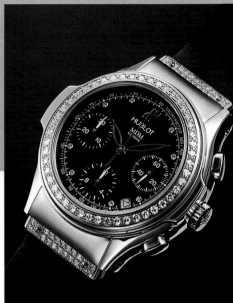

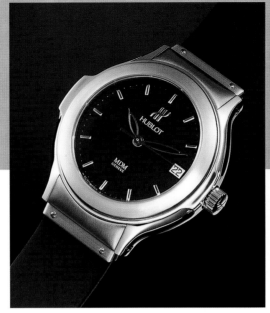

ment created by Frederic Piguet, the mechanical movement or the Eta quartz.

In recognition of special events, Crocco has designed limited, special edition timepieces that dazzle with diamonds, rubies, emeralds or sapphires glowing across the face and bezel. On one timepiece, a lattice cover of fleur de lis opens to show the dial; in another, diamond-studded fish with sapphire blue eyes swim across the watch-face. In another design for the sports enthusiast, a polo player rides gracefully across a colorful cloisonne dial.

Hublot's newest creation is a steel timepiece emblazoned with diamonds, a remarkable achievement as steel is one of the most difficult metals to set with diamonds. But as Suhyda notes, everything Crocco creates is finished to perfection. The Hublot is testimony to this philosophy.

"It's timeless. The original case design is nearly twenty years old yet it is exactly what you envision a watch will look like in the year 2000," says Suhyda, reinforcing that Crocco has achieved his dream of creating the perfect watch for all time.

ABOVE LEFT Elegant model in gold and steel. self-winding mechanical movement with 40 hours power reserve, water-resistant to 50 meters.

ABOVE RIGHT Chronograph in steel with 48 diamonds on bezel and 36 on the end-pieces, self-winding mechanical movement with 40 hours power reserve, water-resistant to 50 meters.

LEFT Classic ladies' models in 18K gold, steel and steel and gold, quartz movement, water-resistant to 50 meters.

INSET Sylvester Stallone seen wearing a Hublot.

LONGINES

*L*ong summer days spent lingering on the veranda, breezing along country roads in a convertible, soaring into the sunset in a bi-plane, hoisting the mainsail on a private yacht, spending an evening playing golf at the country club… this is the amber-hued life of Longines, the watchmaker which since 1832 has created high quality timepieces that define active and classic elegance. Those who wear Longines yearn for romance and the ease of a slower-paced time. Reviving the essence of days gone by is effortless for Longines, a watchmaker which has written significant pages in watchmaking history. Longines is one of the few watchmakers to make its mark on each significant stage in the advancement of the wristwatch, from the moment founder Auguste Agassiz established his workshops in

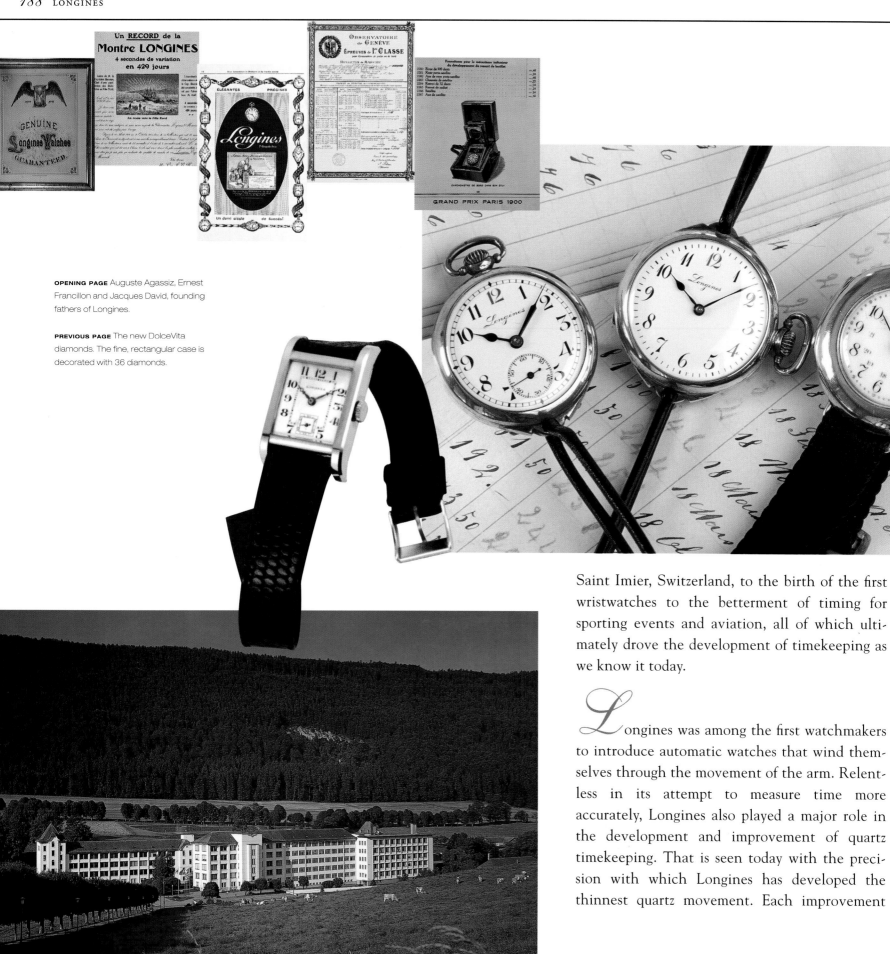

OPENING PAGE Auguste Agassiz, Ernest Francillon and Jacques David, founding fathers of Longines.

PREVIOUS PAGE The new DolceVita diamonds. The fine, rectangular case is decorated with 36 diamonds.

Saint Imier, Switzerland, to the birth of the first wristwatches to the betterment of timing for sporting events and aviation, all of which ultimately drove the development of timekeeping as we know it today.

*L*ongines was among the first watchmakers to introduce automatic watches that wind themselves through the movement of the arm. Relentless in its attempt to measure time more accurately, Longines also played a major role in the development and improvement of quartz timekeeping. That is seen today with the precision with which Longines has developed the thinnest quartz movement. Each improvement has received serious recognition; in fact, Longines received ten World's Fair Grand Prizes and twenty-eight gold medals, more than any other watchmaker in the early days of watchmaking.

For its 130th anniversary, in 1997 Longines presented a trio of vintage timepieces featuring a chronometer, a chronograph and a world time watch in a limited edition of 999. Reproduced to nearly exact specifications, each timepiece is a celebration of the watchmaker's incredible history which dates to 1832, when Auguste Agassiz first began producing timepieces. It was his nephew, Ernest Francillon, who established the name Longines in 1867, naming the company

FACING PAGE

TOP (LEFT TO RIGHT) Longines registered its trademark hourglass with wings in 1889, recorded as the first trademark in the watch industry; Recognition of Captain Bernier's expedition to the North Pole, 1904-05; Advertisement testifying to Longines' precision record obtained from the Concours Observatory, 1920; Chronometer "express Moncarch," circa 1910.

CENTER Gentleman's wristwatch from 1925, white gold, calibre 10.26.

RIGHT Three early ladies' wristwatches. Silver, metal, gold with the calibre 11.62 and 11.62N.

BOTTOM The Longines factory in St. Imier, Switzerland.

THIS PAGE

TOP The first Conquest, 1954.

CENTER The modern Conquest, VHP Perpetual Calendar, in two-tone with a white face, in steel with a blue face.

BELOW (left)The assessment of the Longines precision record on an advertising poster by René Bleuer, 1945. (**RIGHT**) Conquest collection advertisement by René Bleuer, 1955.

after the long meadows surrounding the workshops. Francillon also trademarked the Longines logo, the hourglass with wings, in 1889 — recorded as the first trademark in the watchmaking industry.

Longines' celebration of its past is ongoing through its collections and its devotion toward preserving its history. Just last year, Longines honored its most famous watch designer, Charles Lindbergh, with the Lindbergh Spirit Collection. Shortly after becoming the first pilot to fly solo across the Atlantic, the seasoned aviator sketched his improvements to the chronograph, and in 1931 Longines completed his plans.

Longines' accumulated technology and elegant watches continue to live on today through its contemporary collections: La Grande Classique, DolceVita, and Conquest. At Longines, every style of timepiece has at one time made its mark before returning to kindle the fires of nostalgia in new generations …

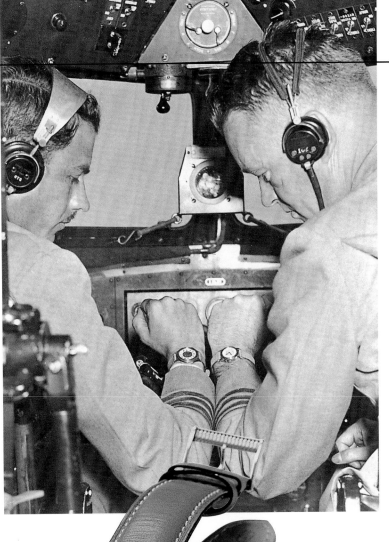

Operating under a new direction since 1995, Longines U.S. is one of several watchmakers under The Swatch Group U.S., formerly known as SMH (U.S.), Inc., that includes Omega, Rado, Hamilton, Tissot, Pierre Balmain, CK, Calvin Klein and, of course, Swatch. The worldwide group is guided by President Nicholas Hayek, who has infused new life into each watchmaker by strengthening brand image, identity and independence.

In the '20s and '30s, Longines was known for its beautiful rectangular watches. Therefore, the 1997 entrance of Longines' DolceVita, which revived this shape, was quite spectacular.

DolceVita's promise of the sweet life lured many to the sleek timepiece even before a moment of advertising had alerted the world to its introduction. DolceVita is sleek and sophisti-

ABOVE LEFT Peter Van Horn Weems and Charles Lindbergh, 1948.

ABOVE In tribute to its founder, Longines created the Francillon Collection of all-mechanical, beautifully crafted timepieces, Shown here, Automatic Chronograph and Automatic, in steel. The striking design features midnight blue numerals and leather strap.

LEFT Examples of the Avigation collection, introduced by Longines in 1997 in tribute to aviator Peter Van Horn Weems who corroborated with Longines in 1923. Shown here, an automatic and automatic chronograph, with white dials, luminous hands, and pale brown leather strap. Water-resistant to 30 meters.

ABOVE La Grande Classique. The timepieces feature an ultra-thin, 1.4 mm quartz movement.

TOP RIGHT The Longines DolceVita collection boasts a modern design that captures the essence of past glory days. In men's and women's sizes, with a polished steel or leather strap.

cated with roman numerals stretching elegantly across white, blue, gray or rose faces housed in steel. The collection has expanded to include diamonds, chronographs and automatics, as well as styles in 18-karat gold.

Today, Conquest is reemerging as Longines' latest introduction to a new age of watch aficionados. The Conquest is a product of the '50s, of a time when living life to the fullest was all important. Over the years, its striking design has been continuously modified to match prevailing trends and has established it as a firm favorite with watch lovers the world over.

"Longines' designers consciously set out to create a watch geared precisely to the ethos of the nineties, a watch that would combine sportiness with the subtle touch of understatement and elegance that is expected today," says Longines U.S. President Michael Benavente.

*B*y embracing its history, Longines has carved a unique position in a watchmaking business that has been scrambling over the past decade to create sports watches for a generation that has grown up driving sports utility vehicles, exploring the outer reaches of the world and increasingly venturing into extreme sports. For over a century at the forefront of technological advances, Longines manages to match the elegance of business attire, evening wear and casual wear with simplicity and grace. "We are happy to be in this market segment in which we foresee the biggest growth potential for the future," says Benavente.

Longines' approach reflecting classic and active elegance is very successful. The best selling collection at the moment is La Grande Classique, thin classic elegant quartz watches whose spartan faces and roman numerals are a perfect tribute to classicism. "There really is an interest in this look," notes Benavente. "We are selling La Grande Classique watches to people who have never been exposed to the classics. They honor sure values and timeless styles not dependent upon fashion cycles."

MOVADO

Excellence in design. A dedication to Swiss craftsmanship. The quest for technological innovation. The Movado philosophy is as valid today as it was back in 1881, when young watchmaker Achille Ditesheim founded the company that later became Movado in the Jura mountain village of La Chaux-de-Fonds, Switzerland. In 1905, Ditesheim's firm was awarded the Gold Medal for quality, creativity and design at the famed Liege Exposition in Paris. That same year, the company adopted the trademark name "Movado," an Esperanto word meaning "always in motion." It proved to be a prophetic choice: since then, Movado has earned 99 patents and more than 200 international awards for innovation in watch design and time technology. Today, Movado watches are exhibited in the permanent collections of prominent

OPENING PAGE In 1881, at the age of 19, Achille Diteshiem founded the company that was to become Movado in La Chaux-de-Fonds, Switzerland.

PREVIOUS PAGE Safiro, from the Movado Museum Sapphire Collection. A contemporary new case design with distinctively squared lugs frames the legendary black Museum dial defined by a solitary dot at 12 o'clock.

ABOVE (LEFT) Like its inspiration, the Polyplan, the sportive new all-steel Eliro bracelet watch features a case and sapphire crystal curved to follow the wrist for elegance and comfort. **(RIGHT)** The ladies' all-steel Eliro is shown here with a diamond-set bezel.

TOP RIGHT The 1912 Polyplan wristwatch represented an innovation in time. It featured a movement created on three levels to fit inside the case curved to follow the wrist.

BOTTOM RIGHT In 1998, the all-steel Vizio chronograph was introduced in bright, bold new color variations.

BELOW A Movado Kingmatic wristwatch made in 1965. Its automatic movement featured a central rotor and 17 jewels; a 1981 ad for the ladies' "Museum Imperiale."

museums on five continents. From the early Movado Polyplan with its revolutionary movement, to the Movado Museum Watch with its legendary single-dot dial, to the new family of automatic Kingmatics and the technologically advanced Viziomatic watch, Movado timepieces continue to win world renown for their superior engineering, unique beauty and timeless design.

During the early years of the twentieth century, Movado led the way in creating a miniaturized movement and popularizing the petite bracelet watch. By 1910, Movado's original designs for ladies' watches reflected the turning point of an age, as popular tastes in fashion shifted from the pendant watch to wrist-worn timepieces.

Innovations quickly succeeded one another. In 1912, Movado created a wristwatch that would remain ahead of its time for decades: The Polyplan, an elongated, rectangular, highly curved wristwatch. Its revolutionary movement, for which Movado received a patent, was uniquely constructed on three levels to fit

into the case which was curved to hug the natural contour of the wearer's wrist. Introduced in 1998, the quartz-precise Movado Eliro, with its curved rectangular case, stands as a proud heir to the original Polyplan design.

In 1926, the Ermeto pocket watch caused quite a stir in watchmaking circles as the first made-for-travel timepiece. The capsule-shaped case, often intricately enameled and exquisitely jeweled, slid open to reveal, then shut to protect the dial. This sliding motion wound the automatic movement — another revolutionary and patented Movado design.

In 1956, the Kingmatic was introduced and honored with prizes for its automatic movement and sweeping seconds hand, both driven from a central rotor — an

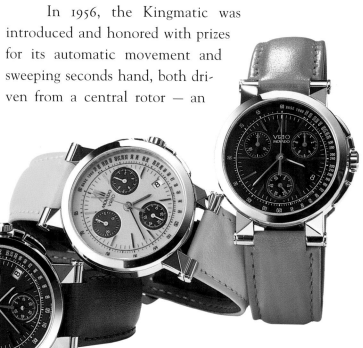

advancement that increased precision and represented a significant achievement in technology. Successful from the start, Kingmatic became the standard Movado model of the late 1950s and 1960s, considered the golden age for Swiss watchmaking. Movado has renewed the inspiration behind this original watch series, reinterpreting it for the next century, with the 1998 introduction of a new automatic line, including Diver and Chronograph models, that proudly bears the Kingmatic name.

*V*izio, launched in 1996, is now the luxury division within the Movado brand. A watch of distinctive contemporary design – the name means "vision" in the international language of Esperanto – Vizio is distinguished by its signature "door-hinge" bracelet with "circular finish" push-button deployment clasp.

Viziomatic, the newest Vizio model, is equipped with the latest development in quartz technology: a self-powered, battery-free quartz movement. Natural, everyday motions of the wrist keep the Viziomatic movement wound, much the way an automatic watch works. The mechanical

ABOVE Reminiscent of their namesakes, the 1950s Movado Kingmatic series, the new Kingmatics all feature precise Swiss-engineered automatic movements. Water-resistant to 50 meters, these watches are crafted in solid stainless steel with black Arabic dials and date displays. Both bracelet and strap models are offered, most in three sizes.

TOP LEFT The all-steel Vizio chronograph on Cordoba calfskin strap. The black dial sports green accents.

BOTTOM LEFT A new Movado ad featuring Pete Sampras, pictured here, juxtaposes his accomplishments as a modern tennis legend, winning titles and setting records in his sport, with the records Movado has attained in watchmaking design and technology.

BELOW The Viziomatic incorporates a breakthrough in quartz technology. Mechanical energy derived from the movement of the wearer's wrist is transformed into stored electrical energy which powers the watch. There's no battery to replace!

energy produced by the motion of the arm is converted into stored electric energy which powers the watch. With a remarkable 100-day power reserve, the Viziomatic requires manual rewinding only if it is not worn for at least 100 days.

The Movado Watch Company is most famous for its celebrated "Museum" watch dial, designed in 1947 by artist Nathan George Horwitt. Horwitt's inspiration was rooted in the beginnings of the modern design movement and the international artists who founded the Bauhaus School in 1919. "Simplicity, tastefulness, function" was their dictum, and one of its purest expressions became the black watch dial defined by a solitary dot. "We do not know time as a number sequence," Horwitt said, but by the position of the sun as the earth rotates. Hence a gold dot at 12 o'clock symbolizing the sun at high noon, the moving hands suggesting the movement of the earth. At once contemporary and timeless, this watch dial represents design simplicity unrivaled in the history of timekeeping. In 1960, Horwitt's original design was selected by the Museum of Modern Art for its permanent collection. It was the first watch dial ever awarded this distinction. The name, the Museum

Watch, derives from this recognition. Today, the artistry and historical importance of numerous Movado watch designs are recognized in prominent museums on five continents, and Horwitt's quest for purity of design has inspired an entire collection of Movado Museum watches.

The celebration of art and design that is the essence of the Movado watch brand was further enhanced by the extraordinary works commissioned for the Movado Artists' Series, beginning in 1987. To date, internationally renowned artists Andy Warhol, Yaacov Agam, Arman, James Rosenquist, Max Bill and Romero Britto have each shared their unique visions of time through the design of these limited edition, highly colorful and collectible watches. Some may be found on display in prestigious museums around the world.

Continually pushing the art form of watchmaking to new artistic and technological heights, Movado remains "always in motion."

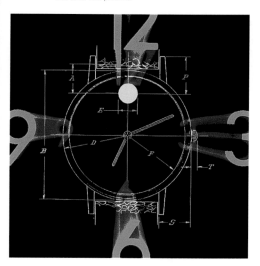

ABOVE The timepiece Pop Art icon Andy Warhol created for the Movado Artists' Series – "Andy Warhol 'Times/5'", produced posthumously in 1987 — is comprised of five separate watches in rectangular cases linked to form a bracelet. Each dial features one of a series of black and white photos of New York City. The edition was limited to 250 pieces.

ABOVE LEFT (LEFT TO RIGHT) The "Lovestar" pocket, bracelet and strap watches by renowned Op and Kinetic artist Agam, created in 1989 for the Movado Artists' Series. Limited respectively to 250 pieces, 100 and 150 pieces.

ABOVE A connoisseur's timepiece, the limited edition gents' Museum Safiro features an open caseback that reveals the exceptional finishing of the mechanical hand-winding movement. Limited to 100 pieces in pink gold and 100 in platinum.

ABOVE About the legendary gold dot Museum watch dial: Nathan George Horwitt, the artist, conceived of a watch without numbers as an experiment in pure, functional and "uncluttered" design.

LEFT A Museum Classic Strap watch model featuring Horwitt's original dial design with flat dot and stick hands.

OMEGA

*S*peedmaster, Constellation, Seamaster and De Ville are legendary names indelibly bound to Omega. In 1848, at La Chaux-de-Fonds, the twenty-three year old Louis Brandt hung out for the first time the sign of his *Comptoir d'établissage* where he produced watches with silver cases and clockwork mechanisms. The production of the Speedmaster—which was first worn on the Moon exactly 30 years ago (July 21st, 1969)—started at the beginning of 1957 but it was only in 1958 that it was launched on the market. This watch was presented as "the new chronograph with tachometer and productometer fit for science, industry and sport". A slogan which has proven to be very prophetic.... Three generations of Speedmaster interact with one another and represent more than forty years of history. In 1964, on September the 29th, the Norman M. Morris Corp. of New York, then the Omega agent in the United States, received an "amazing" order: the request for twelve Speedmasters without strap written on paper headed "NASA Manned Spacecraft Center, Gemini & flight Support Procurement Office Houston Texas"...

Although nearly all watch lovers know this story, it is worth recalling it briefly. In 1964, on September 29TH, two NASA technicians incognito went to Carrigan's, a well-known watch shop in Houston, to buy five chronographs of five different brands. They bought twelve Speedmasters "to test and evaluate them."

The American Space Center wanted to test the chronographs with the possibility of giving them to the astronauts who were to walk in space. A long series of tests were carried out (heat, cold vacuum, humidity, atmosphere saturated with oxygen, crash, acceleration, decompression, overpressure, vibrations, noise) but only the Speedmasters succeeded where all the other tested models failed.

Then a series of tests aimed at verifying the quality of a larger number of Speedmasters began.

The second lot of Speedmasters were so highly accurate that NASA decided at last, on April 1966, to reveal the story to Omega. However, during two previous Mercury Atlas missions some astronauts had already worn a Speedmaster (Walter Schirra in 1962 and Gordon Cooper in 1963) even if on those occasions no space walks had been planned.

PREVIOUS PAGE NASA Space Mission Series of the Omega Moonwatch Speedmaster, the chronograph adopted by NASA for the Apollo XI Mission to the moon. The American Space Center chose it after having anonymously bought and later tested, the best chronographs of that time. Tests showed that only Omegas higher quality standards met space requirements.

ABOVE The Omega Speedmaster tested by NASA.

The NASA engineers wrote in their brief report: "We carried out functioning and simulation tests on the three Omega chronographs; according to the results they have been approved and given to the three members of the GT-3 crew." The astronauts were Grissom and Young who took off on March 23rd 1965. The Speedmaster worked perfectly.

In 1969, Neil Armstrong, the first man to set foot on the Moon, left his Speedmaster inside the lunar module for safety reasons as the clock aboard was out of order. Buzz Aldrin was therefore the first man to walk on the Moon wearing the Speedmaster (which was unfortunately stolen from him years later). Four months after the Moonwalk, the first of a long series of Speedmaster special editions was launched. It was realized in 18K gold and the first production model was given to Richard Nixon, the President of the United States. The promise made in 1961 by John Fitzgerald Kennedy to American people had become a reality. Man had indeed reached the Moon.

Omega proudly used the space vocation of its Speedmaster for its advertising but this hurt the sensitivity of an American watchmaker who put a great deal of pressure on NASA stating the importance of supporting the national industry. Such pressures forced the NASA administrative manager to explain the reasons for that choice to the Senate of the United States of America during a special hearing. Senators wisely preferred giving the astronauts a high quality chronograph, thus obliging the national watchmaking industry to accept the inevitable since at that time, at least, it was not competitive enough. However the industry did not resign itself and started to work hard to try to design a chronograph fit for space missions. In 1978 they presented their latest watch, but a new series of tests showed

LEFT The movement equipping the Moonwatch is the Omega caliber 1863 mounted on 17 rubies and working at 21,600 vibrations per hour. It can be easily viewed through a little window opened on the bottom. This chronograph has preserved its extraordinary characteristics of strength and reliability throughout the years.

BOTTOM The watches dedicated to various space missions such as the Gemini Mission (space flight with a space walk), the Apollo Mission (flight to the moon with a crew of three astronauts) and the Skylab Mission, are in total twenty-two. On each dial, at 9 oclock, there is the emblem of a NASA mission. It is also worth recalling the reproduction of the original Speedmaster (its production started in 1957 but it was launched on the market the following year) and of a transparent box housing Omega caliber 1861 which can be easily viewed (this is supplied with a special magnifying glass).

once more the higher quality of the Speedmaster, at least as far as the requirements necessary for space missions were concerned. There is no doubt that sponsorship had nothing to do with the issue and that the problem was that NASA needed to have a chronograph fit for space missions. As it turned out, NASA made the right choice because without the Speedmaster the astronauts of the Apollo XIII would not have returned to earth alive. On the Apollo13, after most instruments aboard failed the crew, the Speedmaster was used to time the rocket firing for re-entry into the Earth's atmosphere. For this, NASA honored OMEGA with the most prestigious Snoopy Award.

In 1998, the year of its 150th anniversary, Omega launched two chronographs which seemed to be very different: the Speedmaster Replica and the Speedmaster X-33.

The Replica is the exact reproduction of the first Speedmaster produced in 1957. Its most important characteristics are its arrow-shaped hands, its mat black dial and its satined-steel bezel with an engraved tachometric scale and black enameled numbers.

The original chronograph was "updated" only two years later to meet the new aesthetic requirements: in 1959 its bezel was painted black and its dial got a shape almost identical to the present one.

Further design retouches were to be carried out at the end of the Seventies and the beginning of the Eighties according to the style of the period which was characterized by all kinds of eccentricity, including some electrical watches with digital numbers.

In 1985 Omega had already decided to go back to its origins representing a Speedmaster almost identical to the 1957 edition.

ABOVE Speedmaster Replica. The caliber 1861 is a real pleasure to see and one of the best chronograph calibers in the world. The picture shows the profile of the protusions on the case band designed to protect both the crown and the buttons. The Replica also features an internal case made from soft iron to protect the movement from magnetic fields. Excellent are the overdimensioned swing wheel balance and the gasket of the screwed bottom.

ABOVE CENTER Original Speed master of 1957.

TOP RIGHT For its 150th anniversary Omega presents, for the second time, its first edition producing 150 18K gold Replicas. Its profile recalls the design of the classic Speedmaster.

RIGHT The Snoopy Award. After the Speedmaster rescued the Apollo 13 mission, NASA expressed its deep appreciation and awarded OMEGA its highest distinction, the "Snoopy Award", Snoopy, dressed in a spacesuit, had become somewhat of a mascot for the astronauts after being used as a code name on previous Apollo flights.

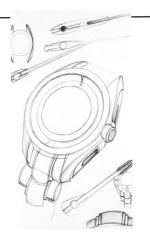  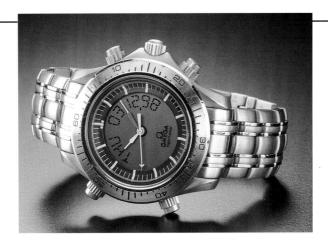

TOP (LEFT TO RIGHT) During five years, several prototypes of the X-33 were designed and realized by Omega and tested in space.

The same design has been adopted by the latest addition to the Omega family: the X-33 designed with and for space voyagers and worn by American astronauts and Russian cosmonauts.

The Speedmaster X-33 was created for a highly specific professional use. At first it had to meet the demand for a professional instrument able to overcome all the known limits of reliability and simplicity of use, and for an instrument ready in all emergency cases (that is the main reason why watches work side by side with on board equipment).

NASA asked Omega if they thought it would be able to produce a multifunctional quartz watch able to withstand space flights. This meant working on aspects of electrical watch-making never before considered.

A few prototypes were produced; the requirements of Russian and American astronauts and flight pilots were taken into consideration and on the basis of their collective comments some changes were made. Since 1992, this chronograph (code name X-33) has been severely tested and in 1998 it was adopted by NASA and the Russian Space program. It took five versions of X-33 to produce the final model, where everything, from the graphics to the shape of the case, from the mechanics of the push buttons to the extraordinary level of the alarm volume was decided, tested and verified according to severe tests.

BOTTOM The X-33 being "water tested" in absence of gravity inside the MIR Space Station.

The Omega Speedmaster Professional X-33 allows maximum variations of one tenth of second a day (36.5 seconds a year) at temperatures ranging from -20°C to +70°C. The X-33 is, all in all, a multifunctional timepiece, which has already been certified by NASA for 100 Space Shuttle Missions and has been chosen by the Russian Space Center as the official MIR watch.

The OMEGA Speedmaster is everywhere: the classic mechanical Speedmaster will be worn by astronauts when working outside the shuttle while the X-33 will remain on-board.

We can end with a short story that underlines the strength of the X-33: a test pilot crashed with his jet and luckily escaped from severe injuries: his X-33, lightly scratched, kept on working.

FUNCTIONS OF THE X-33

The X-33 performs the following functions: hours, minutes and seconds by an analogical display; hours, minutes and seconds with digital display; the possibility to synchronize automatically the analogical hour to the digital one or to set the analogical hour to a time zone different to that of the digital one; a perpetual calendar with digital readouts; digital chronograph accurate to 1/100th of a second with lap function to calculate split times; the possibility to countdown up to 100 hours minus one second with final alarm, after which the "count-down" continues with a positive sign to show that the fixed point has been passed; a watch alarm which sounds every twenty-four hours for 20 seconds (if the alarm is not stopped it starts again after one minute for fifteen seconds, and at this point it is impossible to ignore it because its sound, which reaches the level of 80 decibels, was designed to overcome the noise inside the space shuttle);

BOTTOM The crash of the plane after which the X-33 continued functioning as if nothing had happened.

RIGHT The case and the back of the X-33 are made of titanium. The back, fixed by nine screws, has a very particular shape: it is a real "resonator" (a device used in the past to increase the volume of the sound in acoustic guitars) which increases the sound when the watch is worn.

the long-time chronograph of the remaining Mission Elapsed Time (up to 1,000 days minus one second) with the possibility to use it as a memo function for measuring the intervals between long term scientific experiments; an alarm set for the entire duration of the mission length (which can be scheduled with a precision of one second); the Universal Time (as adopted by scientists all over the world) which can be used to indicate another time zone; an alarm (programmable to a precision of one second) set on the Universal Time; a round central monitor with large liquid crystal digits designed for maximum legibility; the possibility to darken the liquid crystal monitor removing all readouts from it and to recall them by pushing any button; the possibility to recall the Mission Elapsed Time during any function set simply by pushing a specific button; the possibility to illuminate the monitor (in this case, in order to save energy, the second hand stops momentarily); a lithium battery resistant to low temperatures; a titanium case with steel buttons; uni-directional bezel with a steel band showing the graduated scale 1-60; a Kevlar strap with a non slip rubber lining; a curved sapphire glass which provides the best visibility in all light conditions.

The watch is precise to 1/10th of a second a day, independent of temperature changes ranging from -20° C to +70° C.

The Speedmaster, with its "user friendly" design and its easy to recall functions has paved the way for a brand new generation of digital watches.

With the X-33, Omega momentarily ends the historical journey it started with the Original Speedmaster Professional.

COPYRIGHT Augusto Veroni

ABOVE The Speedmaster third generation of is known as the X-33. Its case preserves the old aesthetical design while its hands recall those of the first model of 1957. Generally speaking it is the extraordinary result of the highest modern electronics together with a logic aimed at making it easy to use. It has a uni-directional bezel and easy to hide digital readouts. The X-33 is the result of collaboration between Omega experts and the astronauts.

Moments of the launch of the X-33 at NASA where Omega organized the live satellite link up with the MIR space station.

CENTER TOP Russian Cosmonauts Budarin and Musabayev in the MIR with the X-33.

CENTER Press conference at Space Center Houston with (left to right): Richard Allen, Director of Space Center Houston; Russian Cosmonaut Valery Korzun; Captain Gene Cernan, the last man to walk on the Moon; Gen. Tom Stafford, 4 times in Space, Commander of Gemini 6 and Apollo 10 missions; Michele Sofisti, President of Omega. Russian Cosmonauts Budarin and Musabayev in the MIR with the X-33.

LEFT Colonel Anatoly Solovyev wearing the X-33 during one of his missions in the MIR Space Station.

PARMIGIANI
FLEURIER

One of the best-kept secrets in the watch-making world is out and on his own, creating exclusive and limited masterpieces that define perfection. While the name Michel Parmigiani is not familiar to many, horologists and connoisseurs revere Parmigiani for his devotion to absolute perfection in the creation of timepieces — an obsession that inspires peers to call him "Golden Hands." The release of his first collection in 1996 was anxiously anticipated by aficionados familiar with Parmigiani's reputation as the foremost developer of complex movements for the most esteemed watchmakers in Switzerland. In a virtual apprenticeship to the masters of time, Michel Parmigiani developed solid skills by devoting two decades to the restoration of the world's most important timepieces, including a Breguet "Sympathique"

OPENING PAGE Michel Parmigiani, founder.

PREVIOUS PAGE Gents' Automatic "Memory Time" wristwatch with a second time zone. Case in 18K gold. Gold "Barleycorn" guilloche dial. Aperture at 12 o'clock with Arabic numerals for the second time zone, gold Parmigiani javelin hour and minute hands. Ref. C00821.

ABOVE "Ionica" Hand-wound tonneau gents' wristwatch. Movement with 8-days running time, small seconds hand, calendar and power reserve indicator. Case in 18K gold. Ref. C02022.

BOTTOM "Elegance" Ladies' wristwatches. **(LEFT)** Case in 18K gold, face encircled with brilliants. Lapis lazuli dial. Pebbles style bracelet set with 220 brilliants. Ref. C00522. **(CENTER)** Case in platinum, face encircled with baguette diamonds. Mother-of-pearl dial. Pebbles style bracelet in platinum. Ref. C00505. **(RIGHT)** Case in 18K gold, face encircled with baguette diamonds. Lapis lazuli dial. Pebbles style bracelet set with 112 baguette diamonds. Ref. C00523.

clock from 1820, a celebrated clock that was thought to be beyond repair. Through his work, Parmigiani recovered lost time: his experiences in restoration yielded the lessons of four centuries of watchmaking history, a wealth of knowledge for him to call upon in the creation of his own timepieces.

Restoration itself is a complex business. A restorer must not only learn obsolete techniques from days gone by, he must also try to intuit the very consciousness of earlier watchmakers, who as artisans devoted themselves to each and every timepiece they made. In many instances, unus-

able parts must be recreated in exactly the same manner as they were hundreds of years ago, requiring an exceptional level of sensitivity and meticulousness that few can achieve.

"What the public sees today is the result of work carried out behind the scenes over a period of twenty years. I learned everything from the great masters of the past by restoring their pieces. This is what has provided me the necessary training to give new form to mechanical watchmaking," Parmigiani says.

It was the restoration of one collection that helped forge a critical partnership for Parmigiani, enabling him to start his own house of horology. While working on the "Family Sandoz Foundation" collection, Parmigiani found that he shared similar principles with the group, which is dedicated to preserving Swiss culture. As the one person who had delved furthest into Swiss watchmaking history, Parmigiani was a natural choice of partners for the Foundation.

Parmigiani's decision to first master the art of restoration, then turn to the development of movements for leading Swiss watchmakers in the 1980s, and finally to release his own collection a decade later, reflects a deliberate and serious attitude that holds tradition and technicity in highest regard. Reflecting this philosophy, a small number of watchmakers at the Parmigiani Fleurier factory continue to devote themselves to the restoration of classic timepieces.

*W*hile the pursuit of perfection is the aspiration and passion of every watchmaker, Michel Parmigiani is more earnestly dedicated than most. What other horologists perceive as the final step is for Parmigiani only the beginning. When it comes to developing parts for his timepieces, each is polished to a mirror finish, and then polished four more times before they are of high enough quality to be put into a Parmigiani

ABOVE Gents' automatic skeleton wristwatch with center seconds hand. Case in 18K pink gold. "Geometrical" engraving at four points on the flange. Gold Parmigiani javelin hour and minute hands, blued-steel seconds hand. Ref. 4SQ41.

ABOVE LEFT Gents' automatic wristwatches. **(FAR LEFT)** Case in 18K gold. Greek decoration at four points. Onyx dial. Ref. C00430 **(LEFT)** Case in 18K white gold. Greek decoration at four points of the flange. Lapis lazuli dial. Ref. C00470.

LEFT Gents' automatic skeleton wristwatch with center seconds hand. Case in 18K gold. Flowers engraving at four points on the flange. Blue steel Parmigiani javelin hour and minute hands, blued-steel seconds hand. Ref. 4SQ20.

FAR RIGHT Parmigiani Fleurier manufacture.

TOP OVAL (left to right) Hand-wound ladies' wristwatch. Case in platinum. Face encircled by baguette diamonds. Lapis lazuli dial. Ref. C00503.

CENTER OVAL Ladies "Elegance" wristwatch. Case in 18K pink gold, watchface encircled by brilliants. Onyx dial. Ref. C00541.

BELOW (FAR LEFT) "Crono" Gents' automatic chronograph wristwatch. Ref. C00900 **(CENTER LEFT)** "Minute-Repeater" Gents' wristwatch. Ref. C03520. **(CENTER RIGHT)** "Classic" Gents' automatic wristwatch with date. Ref. C00441. **(FAR RIGHT)** "Elegance" Ladies' wristwatch with baguette diamonds. Ref. C00500.

Fleurier watch. This process applies to all the steel parts down to the screws. "When producing a timepiece, you have to find the technical and aesthetic balance. Many pieces are produced to obtain the optimal quality, but to achieve the optimal aesthetic quality you can produce only a few pieces and these must be very exclusive," Parmigiani opines. "Polished pinion-wings improve the technical functions of a watch. Polished screws improve the aesthetic of the watch."

By coupling the accumulated lessons of watchmaking history with his own fervor as a highly demanding precisionist, Parmigiani has raised the quality of timekeeping to a new level, and he is the only watchmaker to back up his work with a ten-year warranty.

Parmigiani has plans to create a Center of Excellence responsible for the training of young watchmakers. In Parmigiani's workshops in Fleurier, some sixty workers diligently craft the collection of various timepieces and special

orders including pocket watches and elaborate, artful table clocks. Production numbers today reach about 500 pieces a year, allowing the craftsmen the time to "surpass ourselves in everything we do," Michel Parmigiani's credo. Not one part will be used until it measures up to Parmigiani's high standard, and it is the reason that 400 hours will be spent in the assembly of a minute-repeater timepiece. Such attention to detail means that the final masterpieces are affordable only to a small number of those who demand the best and have the means to attain it. So exclusive and tightly controlled is his operation, Parmigiani has designated an "ambassador" in each country to show his timepieces by appointment. In keeping with his philosophy, each ambassador is well versed in even the seemingly mundane tasks involved in caring for a masterpiece. The ambassador supplies a crucial network of collectors, clients and exclusive retailers, guiding the promotion and the distribution of the brand.

*I*t would be easy to assume that Parmigiani has achieved the perfection and excellence for which he strives, yet he maintains that he doesn't have enough time to do everything that he wishes. And where does Parmigiani see the future of watchmaking? "Our collection Parmigiani Fleurier benefits from a great tradition and old knowledge, which I sincerely hope will be transmitted to the next generation."

LEFT Gents' automatic wristwatch. Case in platinum. Greek decoration at four points of the flange. Onyx dial. Ref. C00400.

BELOW LEFT Gents' Automatic "Torus" wristwatch with calendar. Case in 18K gold, "Barleycorn" guilloche dial, charcoal-grey colored printed in black roman numerals. Ref. C00721.

BELOW RIGHT Gents' Automatic "Torus" wristwatch. Calendar at 3 o'clock. 18K gold case. Eggshell-colored dial. Ref. C00799.

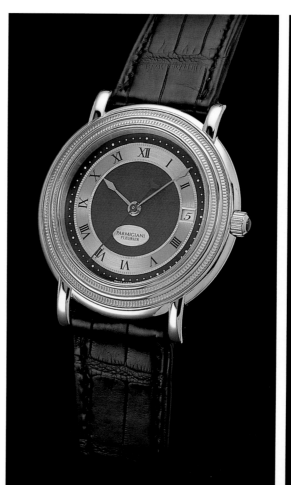

PATEK PHILIPPE

*I*t is often said that rising to the top is easier than staying there, an adage contradicted by the performance of Patek Philippe, whose longevity, prosperity and distinction as the finest watchmaker in the world is without peer. Since its founding by Antoine Norbert de Patek in 1839, Patek Philippe has ceaselessly contributed to advances in timekeeping: as the creator of the first known Swiss wristwatch in 1868, the first perpetual calendar wristwatch in 1925 and as a pioneer in quartz timekeeping starting in 1948. That year, Patek Philippe developed the first fully autonomous, portable quartz clock. A similar clock was presented by Mayor Willy Brandt to President John F. Kennedy when he visited Berlin in June 1963. This unique clock — whose three dials indicate the time in Washington, Moscow and

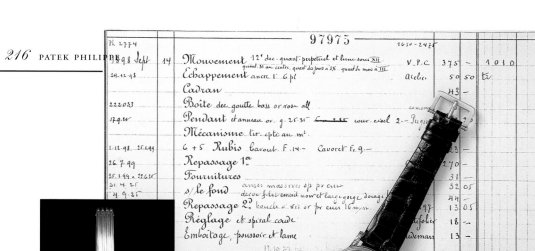

OPENING PAGE Philippe Stern, President of Patek Philippe, admires a timepiece from the Neptune sports collection. Philippe Stern is the third generation of the Stern family to have owned Patek Philippe since 1932. It is the family's commitment to maintain the independence of Patek Philippe in order to preserve its unique standard of watchmaking.

PREVIOUS PAGE The Calatrava ref. 3919 remains the company's most popular wristwatch. The distinctive design with the hobnail patterned bezel was inspired by the company's original Calatrava design introduced in 1932.

ABOVE The first known Swiss wristwatch was commissioned by Countess Kosewicz in 1868.

ABOVE CENTER The first ever perpetual calendar with moon phase wristwatch was completed in 1925. This unique timepiece was created from a ladies' pendant timepiece which was first produced in 1898.

ABOVE OVALS The founders of Patek Philippe; Antoine Norbert de Patek, a Polish businessman who decided to create the finest watchmaking company in the world, and at right, Adrien Philippe, a brilliant French watchmaker who invented the keyless winding system.

CENTER (LEFT) The original 1932 Calatrava wristwatch. This universally recognized design has become a classic. **(RIGHT)** Today, Patek Philippe produces over 24 different models within the Calatrava collection. Shown here is one of the latest versions: ref. 5026.

Berlin — was used in conjunction with the "hot line" telephone and teleprinter linking the White House to the Kremlin.

The Patek Philippe style is known for its subtlety. A Patek Philippe watch never overwhelms; rather, each timepiece reflects understated refinement and elegance that will appeal for generations to come. Testimony to this is the steady popularity of the Calatrava. Created in 1932, today it is Patek Philippe's top-selling watch. Styled for lasting appeal and handcrafted to tell the time accurately for years, the unmatched quality of the Patek Phillipe watch is valued by collectors and experts worldwide. The world's most expensive wristwatch sold at auction is a Patek Philippe original: a unique 1939 complicated watch in platinum with a minute repeater, perpetual calendar and moonphase, which fetched $1.7 million in 1996.

From the moment that Antoine Norbert de Patek established his company, he set the standard for excellence in horology. An astute businessman, Patek was the first to offer collections of watch styles for sale, an inspired deviation from the custom of the time, in which a single watch

would be commissioned from an independent watchmaker. Patek and the exceptional watchmaker Adrien Philippe soon formed a partnership that secured the company's position as a leader in horology. Today, Adrien Philippe is recognized for developing the winding crown, a landmark in wristwatch innovation, which took the place of easy-to-lose keys as the method for winding the movement and thrust the art of timekeeping into the twentieth century.

$\mathcal{A}$lthough Patek Philippe continued its advances in timekeeping accuracy, like many other businesses it was dealt a harsh blow by the Great Depression. In response, Patek Philippe set out to find a sound investor to purchase the company while maintaining its ideals. In 1932, two brothers, Charles and Jean Stern, who had long supplied dials to Patek Philippe, took over ownership and management of the company. Patek Philippe found in the Stern family unequivocal support for its tradition of watchmaking as well as the means to assure that no cost would be spared in the continuing creation of the most accurate, sophisticated watches in the world.

Today under the direction of Philippe Stern, Geneva's last independent watchmaking company carries this commitment into the next millennium. As a family-run operation, Patek Philippe gives its watchmakers the freedom to

FAR LEFT A new complicated watch for ladies with phases of the moon and a small seconds hand indication in 18K white gold. A cabochon sapphire on the winding crown adds a delicate touch to a sophisticated timepiece.

LEFT Known to watch connoisseurs and collectors as a masterpiece, the ref. 5016 is the most complicated wristwatch produced regularly by Patek Philippe. It combines all the complications that constitute the enthusiast's dream: a tourbillon, a minute repeater, a perpetual calendar with fly-back date hand, and the phases of the moon. The magnificent movement can be admired through a sapphire crystal caseback.

BELOW For the first time in its history, Patek Philippe has introduced a complicated wristwatch in a steel case with a sapphire crystal caseback into its current collection. The self-winding movement has a power reserve, date, moon phase and small seconds hand.

ABOVE Also shown on the cover, ref. 5059, combines advanced technology with the elegance of a long lost era. The beautiful movement is housed in an 18K white gold case reminiscent of the hunter-style pocket watches of the last century. By opening the back case cover, it can be viewed through a sapphire crystal.

CENTER This is the latest useful complication wristwatch from Patek Philippe ref. 5036/1: an annual calendar mechanism with day, date, month, phases of the moon and power reserve indicator. The annual calendar automatically adjusts for months with days of 30 or 31. The 18K yellow gold bracelet and case has a sapphire crystal back through which the patented, award-winning movement can be seen.

RIGHT In the 1920s, chronographs became associated with the ever increasing speed of cars, boats and aircraft, and gained popularity as the sportsman's watch. The ref. 5070 revives the racing era with square buttons, large 18K gold case and black tachometer dial in the style of Patek Philippe's pre-1950s chronographs.

work as long as is necessary: nine months to craft even the simplest watch; up to two years to fashion the most intricate complicated watch. Patek Philippe's insistence on incomparable craftsmanship and precision technology begets a painstaking process of research, testing and development. Exercising close oversight of production, the company makes a significantly larger proportion of each of its watches in-house than any other watchmaker — from the crafting and polishing of the small parts that power the movement to the manufacture of the cases and bracelets. The unsurpassed excellence of Patek Philippe craftsmanship is recognized by the highest official rating in watchmaking: the Geneva Seal. Patek Philippe is the only watchmaker whose entire line of mechanical movements qualifies for this distinction.

Much of Patek Philippe's fame centers on its collection of complicated timepieces. The latest complicated watch from Patek Philippe, reference 5059, combines the most advanced techniques in the art of watchmaking in an elegant case reminiscent of the hunter-style pocket watches of the last century. The perpetual calendar movement, which automatically

adjusts for leap years, incorporates a rare complication known as a retrograde or fly-back date-hand. This appears on the dial as a semicircle of numbers indicating the days of the month. At the end of the month, the date-hand flies back, stopping precisely, without causing any friction in the movement. The same mechanism was originally developed for the Calibre 89, the world's most complicated timepiece, which sold at auction in 1989 for $3.2 million.

The brilliant intricacy of the Patek Philippe movement is best observed through the sapphire crystal caseback of reference 5016. The company's most complicated wristwatch, collectors regard it as the ultimate example of the watchmaker's craft. The manually wound movement incorporates a tourbillon, minute repeater, and perpetual calendar with fly-back date hand and phases of the moon. Taking more than two years to build, each watch bears its own rating-certificate issued by the Geneva canton after three weeks of independent testing.

TOP LEFT Ref. 5055 provides the wearer with useful complications such as the date, seconds, phases of the moon and a precise power reserve indicator. The power reserve indicator is particularly useful. If the watch is not worn for a couple of days, the indicator lets the owner know exactly how many more hours the watch will run until it requires rewinding.

ABOVE The coveted Geneva Seal is the highest official recognition of excellence in watchmaking. Patek Philippe is the only watchmaker whose entire production of mechanical movements qualify for the Seal. Twelve strict technical requirements relating to the manufacturing of the movement have to be met in order for the distinguished stamp to be awarded.

LEFT Ladies' Travel Time watches shown here in 18K white and rose gold on leather straps. This ingenious, yet simple-to-use complicated watch has a dual time-zone mechanism which indicates local and home time.

Significant advances, such as Patek Philippe's first wristwatch, have been inspired by women; the first perpetual calendar complicated wristwatch was fashioned from a woman's complicated pendant. It is perhaps for this reason that Patek Philippe is one of the few makers of complicated ladies' watches. A recent addition is the Travel Time watch that displays two time zones.

*I*n recent years, Philippe Stern has expanded the collection by developing a series of useful complications, perfectly suited for those who haven't yet graduated to tourbillons, minute repeaters and retrograde calendars but who want to begin exploring the world of complications.

Patek Philippe launched this concept in 1994 with the introduction of reference 5015, a self-winding wristwatch with power-reserve indicator and phases of the moon. Extremely precise, the moon phase takes 122 years and 45 days to accumulate the error of a single day. Next was the annual calendar reference 5035, awarded the prestigious "Watch of the Year" award in 1996. The patented movement is the first self-winding calendar watch in the world to require resetting only once a year (in February). The latest addition to this collection is reference 5036/1, which has a power reserve and moon phase incorporated into the annual calendar mechanism.

A new chronograph, reference 5070, is inspired by the company's square-buttoned chronographs of the 1930s and 1940s. This chronograph is of particular interest to collectors because it revives a style much sought after at auction.

While the Calatrava is Patek Philippe's longest running, continuously sold line, each timepiece in the company's various collections has its own impressive story.

The company's first sports collection, the Nautilus is an impressive feat of technological engineering. During development in 1976, engineers took on the task of

creating a robust case to house the intricate, sensitive, self-winding movement, allowing it to withstand the pressure and shock of diving, swimming and similar athletic activities. The result is the unique case, carved from a single block of gold or steel that solidly and snugly fits together like a porthole. Taking another step forward, Patek Philippe extended the collection with the Aquanaut line. This contemporary sports watch has a unique strap, which took over a year to develop. Comprised of over twenty different materials, the composite strap is extremely durable and has been certified by the Food and Drug Administration as hypo-allergenic.

Answering the desire of those seeking a watch strong enough to withstand daily use and stylish enough for the most elegant of social occasions, Patek Philippe three years ago introduced its Neptune line. Durable and water-resistant, the Neptune can also be a beautiful piece of jewelry, with many models featuring handcut gems on the dial and bracelet.

The company's Gondolo collection finds its inspiration in the Art Deco period of the 1920s. Many of the current rectangular and square watches can trace their origins to early Patek Philippe watches from this era. The name itself pays tribute to the Rio de Janeiro firm of Gondolo

ABOVE LEFT Man's 18K yellow gold Neptune bracelet watch which is part of a sports collection introduced in 1996. The striking design, decorated with engine-turned rays on the wide bezel and repeated on the bracelet links, displays the precision and detail of Patek Philippe's craftsmanship. Practical for sports-wear because of its robust construction, yet perfect as a dress watch, the Neptune watches are ideal for men and women who lead an active lifestyle.

ABOVE Two examples of exquisitely jeweled ladies' Neptune watches. Each is decorated with the finest diamonds, individually cut and set by Patek Philippe's own jewelers. The dials of these watches are decorated with mother-of-pearl and pavéd diamonds for a feminine and elegant look.

LEFT The Aquanaut with a steel bracelet to complement its steel case and unique textured black dial. The face is decorated with Arabic numerals in white gold; the hour and minute hands have a luminous coating for enhanced visibility in the dark. Water-resistant to 120 meters, this model has a self-winding movement with a date and sweep seconds hand.

ABOVE (LEFT) The men's Gondolo ref. 5010 manually wound wristwatch with small seconds hand exhibits the pared-down lines and abstract hour markings so favored by Art Deco designers. Shown here in 18K white gold. **(CENTER)** The men's Gondolo ref. 5024 demonstrates the classic elegance of the Art Deco era with its stepped bezel and bold dial. This design was inspired by Patek Philippe's archive collection of original Art Deco watches from the 1930s.

TOP RIGHT AND CENTER Thirty years ago, Patek Philippe introduced a new design of watches called the Golden Ellipse. The elliptical shape draws inspiration from Euclid's principle of perfect proportion. Known as the Golden Section, it underlies the design of much classical architecture and was first used in the construction of the Parthenon. Today it is still recognized as a symbol of harmony and elegance, recreated here as beautiful timepieces for women of discernment. Both of these 18K white gold watches have mechanical movements hallmarked with the Geneva Seal. The strap version, ref. 4931, has a quick change device which makes it simple to change the color of strap. The hand-finished, elaborate bracelet version has the distinctive blue colored gold dial, a creation unique to Patek Philippe.

& Labouriau, who became famous for their Chronometro Gondolo pocket watches, which were made for them by Patek Philippe in the 1920s.

Patek Philippe also has a history of exploring new decorative techniques. One striking example is the Golden Ellipse. Introduced in 1968, the watch immediately made an impact with its shimmery blue face. The dial, in fact, is coated with 18-karat blue-colored gold, a process invented and patented by Patek Philippe. The Ellipse is also noteworthy for its design, based on the Golden Section principle of classical architecture that inspired the Parthenon.

Just as the Ellipse captivates the eyes, Patek Philippe's La Flamme watches curve around the wrist in a perfect fit. Each bracelet of the intricate watch is handmade — the only tools used, a pair of pliers and a pair of hands — and no two are alike. In the 1960s, the design was discovered by chance in a box of beautiful chains and bracelets. However, it was not until the 1980s that goldsmiths mastered the technique to dupli-

cate and craft the sinuous flame-patterned bracelet that gives this collection its name.

Patek Philippe's comprehensive archives, which document every timepiece created since 1839, are testament to the extraordinary contribution the company has made to the world of watchmaking. While technology is advancing at a rapid pace, Patek Philippe stays on top by exploring the newest techniques through its own research and development division and by inspiring its craftsmen to push the limits of the latest technology. Yet the watchmaker continues to finish each timepiece by hand and works ceaselessly to create timepieces of unparalleled accuracy and distinction.

LEFT La Flamme's unique and enduring design is truly a piece of jewelry to be cherished. The extraordinarily supple, flame-patterned bracelet melts onto the wrist for a perfect fit. The reason for such flexibility is that each bracelet is completely hand-made, crafted with a pair of hands and a pair of pliers. Because of this, no two bracelets are alike and each timepiece is a unique piece of jewelry. Seen here is a goldsmith at Patek Philippe creating the links of a bracelet out of 18K yellow gold. It takes three weeks to weave the delicate links of each bracelet. When the bracelet is complete, jewelers hand-set each flawless diamond. Finally, the bracelet is hand-polished. The iridescent mother-of-pearl dial is offset with diamond hour-markers and delicate hands of twisted gold.

PHOTO CREDITS

FRONT AND BACK COVER: Patek Philippe. INTRODUCTION: Parmigiani. p3: Chopard. p6: Girard Perregaux. p7: Hublot. p9: Bedat. p11: Boucheron. p12 Peter Laetsch. p13 Photo of La Vallée de Joux. p15: The Swatch Group. p17: Gerald Genta. p19: Daniel Roth.

BIRTH OF THE WRISTWATCH p20: Audemars Piguet. p21: Audemars Piguet. p22: Chaumet; Vacheron Constantin. p23: Patek Philippe; IWC; Girard-Perregaux. p24: Movado; Concord; Audemars Piguet. p25: Eterna; Oris; Cartier; Movado. p26: Boucheron; Van Cleef & Arpels; Breitling. p27: Audemars Piguet; IWC; Eterna. p28: Van Cleef & Arpels; Piaget. p29: Boucheron; Longines. p30: Oris; Movado; Longines; Eterna. p31: Cartier; Corum; Concord. p32: Movado; Hublot; Ulysse Nardin; Daniel Roth; Corum; Gerald Genta. p33: Jaeger-LeCoultre; Patek Philippe; Vacheron Constantin; Gerald Genta; background Longines. p34: A. Lange & Sohne; Parmigiani Fleurier; Bedat; background Patek Philippe. p35: Breguet; Longines; Panerai; Breitling. p36: Omega; Franck Muller; Patek Philippe. p37: Blancpain; Rolex; Hamilton. p38: Girard-Perregaux; Corum; Audemars Piguet; Patek Philippe. p.39: Blancpain; Girard-Perregaux; Bedat; Eterna; background Audemars Piguet.

DAWN OF A NEW ERA: p41: Hamilton. p42: Piaget; Longines; Eterna; p43: Girard-Perregaux; Corum; Patek Philippe. p44: Piaget; Girard-Perregaux. p45: Swatch; Longines. p46: Longines; Gerald Genta; Swiss Tourism Office. p47: Movado; Hublot; p48: Longines. p49: Concord; Chaumet; Beatles, Piaget; Andy Warhol. p50: Hamilton; Bedat; Girard-Perregaux; Daniel Roth; Longines. p51: Baume & Mercier; Franck Muller; Corum; background Franck Muller. p52: Bertolucci; computer drawing, Franck Muller; Chopard; p53: Breitling; Dunhill. p54: Sarcar; Philippe Charriol; Piaget drawings. p55: Omega; Raymond Weil; Tiffany; Millerio Meller. p56: Daniel Roth; Vacheron Constantin; Movado. p57: Van Cleef & Arpels; Cartier; Matterhorn, Swiss Tourism Office.

AFTER EIGHT: p58: Boucheron. p59: Boucheron. p60: Dunhill; Van Cleef & Arpels; Chaumet. p61: Audemars Piguet; Vacheron Constantin; Van Cleef & Arpels. p62: Piranesi; Breguet; Van Cleef & Arpels. p63: Concord. p64:

Harry Winston; Franck Muller; Rudolph Valentino, Gloria Swanson, Cartier. p65: Audemars Piguet; Cartier; p66: Omega; Concord; Harry Winston; Audemars Piguet; Chopard. p67: Van Cleef & Arpels; Bertolucci. p68: Patek Philippe; Corum; Piaget. p69: Breguet; Omega. p70: Cartier; Chopard; Vacheron Constantin; Chopard. p71: Bulgari; Jaeger-LeCoultre. p72: Bedat; Piaget; Chaumet. p73: Piaget; Bertolucci. p74: Girard-Perregaux; Chopard. p75: Chaumet; Chopard. p76: Parmigiani Fleurier; Girard-Perregaux. p77: Piaget; Blancpain; Hublot. p78: Daniel Roth. p79: Chanel; Harry Winston; Piranesi.

WINNING TIME: p80: Breitling. p81: Breitling. p82: Corum; Eterna; Bell & Ross. p83: TAG-Heuer; Blancpain. p84: Harry Winston; Breguet; Chaumet; Jaeger-LeCoultre; Chaumet. p85: Fortis; Gerald Genta; Omega. p86: Breitling; Rolex; Concord. p87: Hublot; Parmigiani; Piaget; walk in space courtesy of Omega. p88: Daniel Jean Richard; Bell & Ross; skier ESQ; Longines. p89: Franck Muller; Perrelet; Omega. p90: Vacheron Constantin; Eterna; Longines. p91: Longines; IWC. p92: Breitling; Movado; Eterna. p93: Harry Winston; Patek Philippe; Corum. p94: Omega; Chopard; Bell & Ross. p95: Gerald Genta; Omega. p96: Chronoswiss; Breguet; auto driver, Omega. p97: TAG-Heuer; auto race, Chopard. p98: Daniel Roth; TAG-Heuer. p99: TAG-Heuer; Oris. p100: Ebel; Omega; Audemars Piguet; Girard-Perregaux. p101: Hamilton; TAG-Heuer. p102: Longines; Franck Muller. p103: Ebel; Bedat; Fortis.

p106-111: Audemars Piguet. p112-117: Bedat. p118-125: Boucheron. p126-133: Breitling. p134-139: Chaumet. p140-147: Chopard. p148-153: Concord. p154-159: Daniel Roth. p160-165: Gerald Genta. p166-173: Girard Perregaux. p174-179: Hamilton. p180-187: Hublot. p188-195: Longines. p196-203: Omega. p204-209: Parmigiani Fleurier. p210-219: Patek Philippe.

FACING PAGE Introduced in 1996, Vizio is a watch of post-modern design, architectural in feeling. The Vizio collection includes all-steel chronographs and watches crafted in high-grade stainless steel, solid 18K gold or steel and gold, with or without diamonds. Most Vizio models come in four sizes.

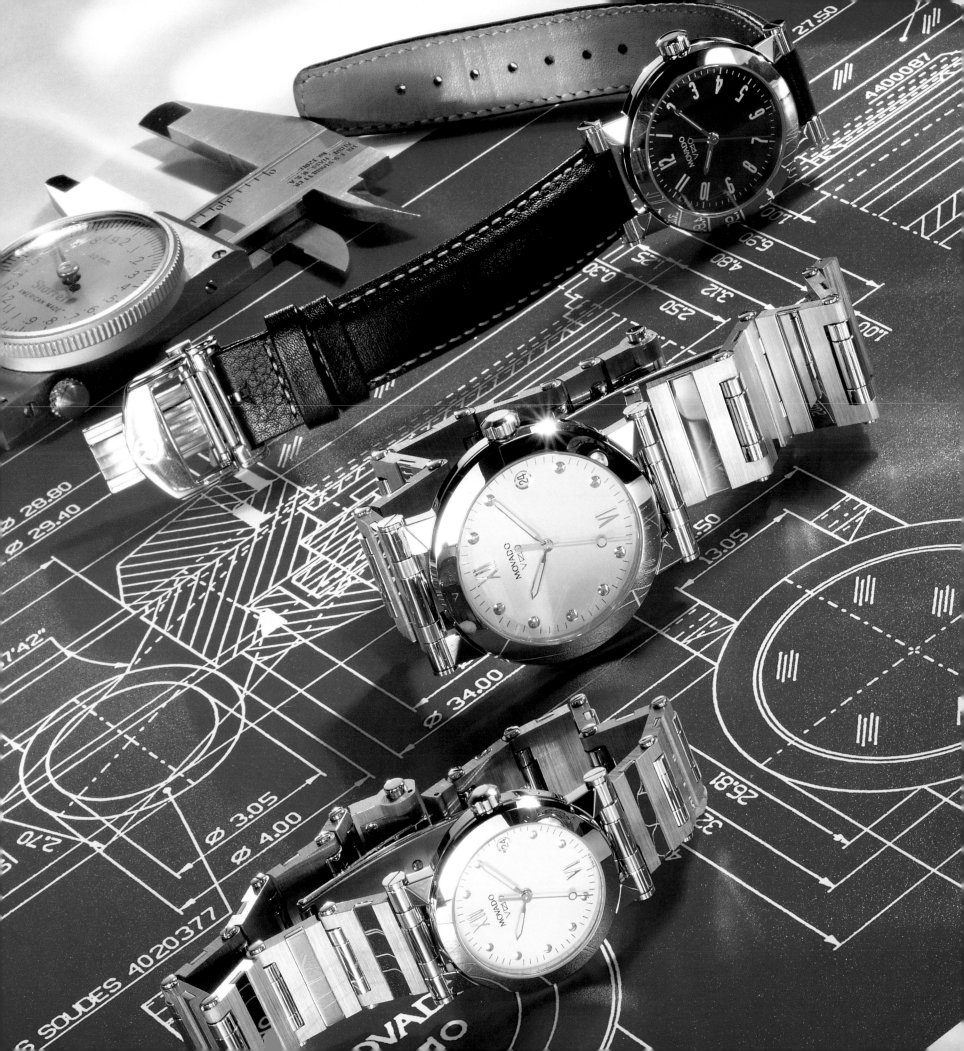

BIBLIOGRAPHY

Barracca, Jader, Gimapiero Negretti, Franco Nencini. Le Temps de Cartier. Wrist International S.r.l., 1989.

Breguet, Emmanuel. Breguet. Watchmakers since 1775. Paris: Alain de Gourvuff, editeur, 1997.

Brunner, Gisbert, Christian Pfeiffer-Belli, Martin K. Wehrli. Audemars Piguet. Masterpieces of Classical Watchmaking. Audemars Piguet,1993.

Brunner, Gisbert, Christian Pfeiffer-Belli. Wristwatches. Atglen, PA: Schiffer Publishing Ltd.,1997.

Brunner, Gisbert L., Marc Sich. Mastering Time. Paris, France: Editions Assouline, 1997.

Cologni, Franco, Gimapiero Negertti, Franco Nencini. Piaget Watches and Wonders. Abbeville Press Publishers, 1994.

Cologni, Franco, Eric Nussbaum. Platinum by Cartier. Triumphs of the Jewelers' Art. Harry N. Abrams, Inc., Publishers, 1995.

de Carle, Donald. Watch & Clock Encyclopedia. New York: Bonanza Books, 1977.

Fritz, Manfred. Reverso. The Living Legend. Jaeger-Le Coultre. Edition Braus, 1992.

Hampel, Heinz. Automatic Wristwatches from Switzerland. Atglen, PA: Schiffer Publishing Ltd., 1994.

Huber, Martin, Alan Banberry in collaboration with Gisbert L. Brunner. Patek Philippe Geneve. Antiquorum, 1988.

Humbert, B. The Chronograph; Its Mechanism and Repair. La Conversion (Switzerland) Editions Scriptar S.A., 1990.

Jespersen, James, Jane Fitz-Randolph. From Sundials to Atomic Clocks. U.S. Department of Commerce, 1977.

Lambelet, Carole, Lorette Coen. The World of Vacheron Constantin Geneve. Scriptar SA/Vacheron Constantin Geneve, 1992.

Lang, Gerd-R, Reinhard Meis. Chronograph Wristwatches to Stop Time. Atglen, PA: Schiffer Publishing, Ltd., 1993.

Landes, David S. Revolution in Time. Cambridge, MA: The Belknap Press of Harvard University, 1983.

Pippa, Luigi. Masterpieces of Watchmaking. Scriptar S.A. / Sperling & Kupfer Editori S.P.A., 1966.

Richter, Benno. Bretiling. The History of a Great Brand of Watches. Atglen, PA: Schiffer Publishing Ltd., 1995.

Sauers, Don. Time for America. Lititz, PA: Sutter House, 1992.

Scarisbrick, Diana. Chaumet. Master Jewellers since 1780. Alain de Gourcuff Editeur, 1995.

Tolke, Hans-F, Jurgen King. IWC, International Watch Co., Schaffhausen. Zurich, Switzerland: Verlag Ineichen,1987.

Von Osterhausen, Fritz. The Movado History. Atglen, PA: Schiffer Publishing Ltd., 1996.

Von Osterhausen, Fritz. Wristwatch Chronometers. Atglen, PA: Schiffer Publishing, Ltd., 1997.

RIGHT Three rectangular wristwatches, yellow gold gadroons, two cabochon rubies, sapphires or emeralds. Boucheron Archives, 1984.